Women, Words & Wisdom

A KENTUCKY COOKBOOK

by

Kim Mitchell / Judith Ralph

10- digit International Standard Book Number 0-9718928-1-4
13- digit International Standard Book Number 978-0-9718928-1-1
Library of Congress Card Catalog Number 2006935454

Cover design and book layout by Asher Graphics

Manufactured in the United States of America

Hen House Press in association with

McClanahan
Publishing House

All book order correspondence should be addressed to:

Hen House Press
4341 Hawesville Rd.
Reynolds Station, KY 42368

E-mail inquiries: jhenhousepress@bellsouth.com
To Order Call: 270-233-4237 or 270-233-4274

Dedication

I dedicate this book to my mother, Emogene Miller Moseley, who has taught me through example to love God and family. My mother taught me to value the morals of the Bible and to strive to live up to what God expects. When I fail, I have only myself to blame. This is called responsibility.

My mother stressed the importance of family and the commitment that one makes when choosing to marry and to have children. If I desired a career that was admirable, if I needed to work to supplement my family's income that was necessary, if I chose and was able to be a stay-at-home mom, that was honorable. Her belief was and is that husband and children are to come before job. She set a great example.

When Mom worked outside the home, it was out of necessity, not to possess a lot of things. My dad, my brother, and I never sacrificed because of her job. For 11 years Mom was employed as secretary at Whitesville Elementary School. She never failed to rise early, before leaving the house, to have a hot meal waiting on the stove for my dad when he came in from work. I remember hearing the washer and the dryer running up into the wee hours of the night.

Mom didn't make a lot of money as secretary at the local elementary school, but my brother and I were seldom home alone. We didn't have all the material things we desired, but we had everything we needed, plus a lot of love.

With all my love to Mom (Dad I love you too!),

Judith Moseley Ralph

Dedication

There is no way this book could ever have been considered except for the influence of my mom, Judy Motley Back. Mom, at 16 you decided to marry your teenage sweetheart. At seventeen you began your family. I would be the first of three children. There were no parenting workshops or marriage retreats to attend. Yet somehow, you knew how to nurture, provide, and protect us.

Today, we children are successful in our own way. We each have college degrees, wonderful spouses, beautiful children and best of all Christ in our lives. You always told us we could do anything and we believed you. When we made disappointing decisions you still stood beside us. When we've had things to celebrate you've been right there with us. Your words of wisdom, guidance, and loyalty continue as I try to parent my own children with the same.

Thank you for offering the best you had, a Christian home, 44 years of marriage to our dad, many delicious meals, and lots of prayers.

Kim Mitchell

Introduction

Kimberly Back Mitchell and Judith Moseley Ralph, co-authors of *A Kentucky Gathering, Recipes & Remembrances*, have once again combined their talents to create a unique cookbook portraying life in Kentucky. Of *Women, Words and Wisdom, a Kentucky Cookbook* is for and about the women in Kentucky. It is a cookbook of reflections of past and present day women, their contribution to the family and to the community. Both young and old alike will be inspired by stories of heartache and of joy, of milestones achieved and of the detailed simplicities in the life of a woman and those who surround her.

And, in addition to these narratives, the cookbook contains a variety of recipes true to Kentucky, including The Famous Doris Ann Cambron's Burgoo founded on the banks of the Ohio River, the ever popular Chocolate Breakfast Gravy and the Golden Whisk Award-winning Pecan Pumpkin Torte. This cookbook will appeal to novice as well as to seasoned cooks in kitchens across America.

Nurturing Hands

It is impossible to say in a few words what could be said about my mother. I could write a book about her. She enjoyed the outdoor things like hunting, looking for herbs to make cough syrup, or picking greens in the spring of the year. She loved to play checkers. I wish I had let her win more often.

She never knew of the luxuries of life. We got electricity in 1948 but it would be years later before we would have indoor plumbing.

Her day would often begin by fixing a breakfast of biscuits and gravy. She made the best biscuits I ever ate. While we were eating breakfast, she would go to the barn and milk the cow.

Mother held my hand many times during my life. I had the pleasure of holding hers in her death. When she took her last breath she squeezed my hand as if to say, "It's ok, I will see you later."

Foy Back

APPETIZERS

The Mitchell Family
From left to right: Daniel, Anthony, Kim, Michael, Ralph

Ralph and I married in college. He was an agriculture major and I was a nursing major. We decided very quickly that we would have to share the homemaking responsibilities. I'll never forget Ralph's first cooked meal. I opened the oven and found a Dominoes Pizza Box.

Andrew's Guacamole

1 large red onion
2 medium tomatoes
2 jalapeño peppers
2 serrano peppers
½ bunch of cilantro
Juice of 1 lemon
Juice of 1 lime
½ tablespoon garlic salt
½ tablespoon fresh-ground black pepper
¼ tablespoon cayenne pepper, optional
3 good size avocados
1 teaspoon mayonnaise
1 teaspoon hot sauce
1 teaspoon Worcestershire sauce

Chop the onion, tomatoes, and peppers finely and place in a plastic mixing bowl. Chop the cilantro and add to the chopped vegetables. Add the lemon and lime juices, garlic salt and peppers and mix well. Peel, deseed and mash the avocados in a separate plastic bowl. Fold in the mayonnaise, hot sauce and Worcestershire sauce thoroughly. Combine the vegetable and avocado mixtures. Place plastic wrap on top of the guacamole mixture and push down to form an airtight seal. Place the lid on the bowl and refrigerate for several hours. Mix well before serving. Serve with tortilla chips.

Andrew Hollifield

Aunt Jean was the first person to get a television in our area. We would go over on Saturday nights and watch wrestling with "Bouncin' Betty." When we finally got our television, we watched Dragnet.

Phyllis Blanton

Artichoke Dip

13¾-ounce can artichoke hearts, drained and chopped
¼ cup salad dressing
4 ounces cream cheese, softened
¼ cup sour cream
¼ teaspoon onion powder
¼ teaspoon garlic powder
1 teaspoon Worcestershire sauce
4 strips bacon, fried and crumbled

Combine the artichoke hearts and the remaining ingredients. Place in a 1½-quart greased baking dish. Bake at 350 degrees for 30 minutes. Serve with crackers.

A Christmas Eve tradition that our family shares in is the meal following the opening of gifts. We call it a meal because Mom prepares so much food but it is actually a variety of finger foods. She has always made many appetizers, both warm and cold and served a delicious punch. Today we continue to celebrate this tradition. The sisters-in-law now add some of their favorite snack recipes to the spread.

Kim Mitchell

Big Sister's
Best Grilling Sauce

½ cup vegetable oil
1 cup vinegar
¼ teaspoon black pepper
2½ tablespoons salt
1½ teaspoons poultry seasoning
1 egg, beaten

Combine all of the ingredients. Use for basting chicken, ribs or pork. Cook the meat on the grill until done.

No one I know loves to grill outdoors more than my oldest sister, Brenda Young. She makes visiting her house so much fun and always finds the most interesting places to visit. We have held outdoor picnics all over the United States from Arizona to Virginia, Tennessee, Florida and of course here at home in the Bluegrass State of Kentucky as Brenda followed her husband's career. I will always enjoy picnicking because of my sister.

Shelia Oliver Thurman

Angel Wings

Mama was 4 years old when her mama died and she always remembered that day. A neighbor woman was there at the house and she said to little Minnie, "Your Mother has died and she has gone to heaven." She took Mama to the bedroom door and opened it. Mama expected to see her mother with wings flying away.

Lorene Leach Wright

Chipped Beef Appetizers

8-ounce package cream cheese
Two 2-ounce packages chipped beef
3 to 6 green onions, chopped
3 tablespoons Worcestershire sauce
1 teaspoon salt
5 to 6 black olives, chopped
2 to 3 shakes jalapeño pepper sauce
One 10-count package flour tortillas

Combine all of the ingredients in a bowl. Spread on flour tortillas and roll up. Refrigerate until firm. Slice each roll into ¼-inch slices.

Buttercup Dressing

2 eggs, beaten
¼ cup self-rising flour
¼ cup lemon juice
1 cup sugar
2 cups pineapple juice
½ bag miniature marshmallows

Combine the first 5 ingredients in a small saucepan. Cook over a medium heat until thickened. Remove from the heat. Add the marshmallows and beat until the marshmallows are dissolved. Refrigerate. This recipe can be used as a dressing for fruit salad, banana salad, etc…

Polly Lindsey

Chocolate Chip Cheese Ball

8-ounce package cream cheese, softened
½ cup butter (no substitutes), softened
¼ teaspoon vanilla extract
¾ cup powdered sugar
2 tablespoons brown sugar
¾ cup miniature semisweet chocolate chips
¾ cup finely chopped pecans
Chocolate graham crackers

Combine the cream cheese, butter and vanilla extract and beat using an electric mixer until fluffy. Add the sugars gradually and beat just until combined. Stir in the chocolate chips. Cover and refrigerate for 2 hours. Remove from the refrigerator and place the cream cheese mixture on a large piece of plastic wrap. Shape into a ball and refrigerate for at least 1 hour. Roll the cheese ball in the pecans just before serving. Serve with the graham crackers. Makes approximately 2 cups.

Joyce Leach

Mothers and Sons

In April of this year, I was honored to have helped in the planning and preparation of my son, Robert, and his fiancé, Kellie Hall's wedding reception. The Chocolate Chip Cheese Ball was one of the foods served and was very well received. Mothers enjoy doing these things for their sons as well as for their daughters.

Judith Ralph

Fancy Gorp
(Good Ole Raisins and Peanuts)

3 cups fruit and nut granola cereal
¾ cup unsalted peanuts or walnuts
½ cup semisweet chocolate chips
½ cup raisins
1 cup peanut butter pieces
1 cup toasted coconut, if desired

Combine all of the ingredients in a serving bowl. Mix well and serve. Makes twenty-three 3-ounce servings.

This recipe was served at one of the many Title I meetings held at Fordsville Elementary School. One facilitator in particular, Edwina Brown, made sure that we as faculty and staff had many good times and lots of good food at these meetings with the students and their parents. Kids loved this healthy treat and so did the adults.

Judith Ralph

To Give Life

When I was considering adoption, I told my friend, Cheryl Richards, that I wanted my child to be of my body; that I wanted to give my child life. In her wisdom, she replied that a child who does not have parents does not have a life. When you adopt a child you give that child life.

Shelia Thurman

Howard Family Barbecue Dip

½ gallon vinegar
2 pounds lard or butter
1 pint lemon juice
1 quart Worcestershire sauce
Salt to taste
Red pepper to taste
4 ounces black pepper
1¼-ounce container garlic powder
Onion powder to taste
1 large onion, chopped
1 lemon, sliced

Combine all of the ingredients in a large kettle. Stir and heat.
This makes enough dip to barbecue 12 to 15 chickens.

Pamela and Barry Howard

In Western Kentucky there is a distinct difference between barbecue sauce andbarbecue dip. Sauce is thick and spicy for flavoring meat, while dip is thin for saturating the meat, yet allowing the smoke flavor to dominate.

Original Party Mix

6 tablespoons butter
2 tablespoons Worcestershire sauce
1½ teaspoons seasoned salt
¾ teaspoon garlic powder
½ teaspoon onion powder
3 cups corn cereal
3 cups rice cereal
3 cups wheat cereal
1 cup mixed nuts
1 cup pretzels
1 cup garlic bagel chips
Gold Fish, optional
Hot sauce, optional

Preheat the oven to 250 degrees. Melt the butter in a large roasting pan in the oven. Add the seasonings. Add the remaining ingredients and stir to coat evenly. Bake, stirring every 15 minutes, for 1 hour. Pour onto paper towels to cool. Store in an airtight container. Makes 12 cups.

Microwave: Cook, 5 to 6 minutes, stirring every 2 minutes.

From Grandma Harrel, Christmas 2003
Heather Litsey

So Easy Cheese Ball

Two 8-ounce packages cream cheese, at room temperature
1 cup shredded Cheddar cheese
Onion salt to taste
Garlic powder to taste
Pecans, chopped

Combine all of the ingredients except the pecans in a bowl until
smooth. Refrigerate for a couple of hours. Form the mixture into
a ball. Roll in the pecans. Refrigerate.

Note: I like to let the cheese ball come to room temperature
before serving. This can be made ahead of time, several days, to let
the flavors blend.

*I made this cheese ball a month before my daughter Jamie's wedding reception and
froze it. The day before the reception I put it in the refrigerator to thaw. Then I
set it out of the refrigerator about three hours before party time to reach room
temperature.*

Joyce Leach

Little Denim Jacket

*When I was a boy three years of age Mam had a Singer treadle
sewing machine. It was time for me to be in bed so I lay
awake watching Mam sew. She was making me a blue denim
jacket with a red flannel lining. She had bought the denim with
egg money. I remember her walking over to the bed and having
me try on that little denim jacket.*

James Lexter Leach

Mar. 7, 1864
    Dear husband,

         I take the present opportunity to inform you that I and the children are well at this time and hope when these lines reach you that they may find you enjoying the same blessing.
         I received a letter from you in the last mail dated the 17th of February and was glad to hear you were in good health but sorrow to hear that you had not received your things that I sent you. I want you to try and get paroled. If there is any chance so that you may come home and stay with me. There is persons here that have been paroled. They are now living with their families.
         You spoke of wanting someone to try and get you out of prison. I know of no way to accomplish your wishes other than for you to take the oath prescribed by the President of the United States. You can inquire of some of the officers, probably they can inform you what course to pursue in this matter or write yourself if it is not contrary to law and if there is any chance for you to come home do not neglect it as I want you to be with us the remainder of our lives and if you can't get off and are exchanged do not re enlist in the rebel service again but try and content yourself the best you can though I know the best—is but poor comfort living as we are living. I do not want you to let anyone know I advised you to take the oath of amnesty as there are some that might not like me to so advise you but I believe it is the best you can do if you will be allowed that at all, and if you take any such steps so do it in a hurry or if you are required to give security I think that you could do that quite easy. I want you to let me know just as soon as possible. I must bring this letter to a close by saying to you that I hope the Lord will enable you to discharge your duty towards—and all mankind and bless me by your return.

                                         Your affectionate and
                                            Devoted wife,
                                         Belinda A. Moseley

         Judy Russell submitted this 142-year-old letter which illustrates how the words so carefully scribed by one woman during an intense moment of desperation determined the course of history for her husband and many generations to follow.

(continued)

John Wesley Moseley, Jr., did in fact petition for amnesty upon the insistence of his wife Belinda and was released from the Yankee prison camp in Rock Island, Illinois. He returned to his home in Ohio County where he lived to be 100 years old. After Belinda's death, John Wesley fathered 3 more children by a second wife, Narcissa Elizabeth Flannigan Kelley Moseley, my great-great grandmother.

Judith Ralph

In this tin-type photo my 3rd great-grandmother, Nancy Westerfield Moseley, is dressed in black mourning clothes. She is commemorating the death of her husband, John Wesley, Sr. in 1879. Household manuals in that time instructed individuals on appropriate mourning etiquette and widows were expected to mourn for 2 full years!

Judith Ralph

Soups

Alzera Allie Estelle Ralph
November 3, 1895 to December 13, 1978
Dynamite

Grandma Allie weighed 1 pound when she was born. They put her in a shoe box for a crib and pinned her to a pillow at night so they wouldn't lose her...DYNAMITE comes in small packages!!!

Bill Ward

November 15, 1983

Dear Little One,

Here it is on a cold fall night and I am so worried about you. I have been concerned from the moment that I first felt you move. You are the most precious thing in my life now and I so want you to know that from the time that you were conceived, you have been a special gift from God to me. I love you with every breath I breathe. Feeling you move and grow inside of me fills me up with excitement with each passing day. I cannot wait until you are born so that I can see you move, see you breathe and feel your warmth. Your brother and sisters are anxious to get to meet you also. They have touched your movement with eyes wide in amazement of the life inside of their mother. Your brother, Josh, wants you to be a boy, poor fellow he is surrounded by females. I want you to be healthy, whether a boy or a girl, and of course I already know you are beautiful

I pray for your sake that the birth will go easily. I want everything perfect for you. Life has a way of dealing the cards as it wants them played. There is so much dissatisfaction within the family at this time because I am bringing another baby into the world. But I won't let this negative feeling ever touch you. To be a small, precious, unknowing baby is a gift only God can give. It is a shame that you will have to grow up and know how cold and hard the world can be. I want to protect you from all of those ugly and harsh facts. I want you to be able to be blemish free and as naïve as you are at birth.

You were conceived through my deepest love for your father and I want you to know that. I have no way of knowing what the future holds for either of us, but at this moment in time you must know what a great miracle it is to be able to hold your life inside of me. To realize that one day you and I will be able to meet for the first time. I only pray that at your birth, everyone will be as proud and eager to love you as I have been.

Your Mother,

Debra Tron

Cabbage Patch Soup

6 carrots, chopped
28-ounce can whole tomatoes, chopped
10-ounce package shredded cabbage
2 green peppers, chopped
1 bunch celery, chopped
Water
1-ounce envelope onion soup mix

Combine the carrots, tomatoes, cabbage, green peppers and celery in a pot. Add enough water to cover the vegetables. Season with the onion soup mix. Bring to a boil and boil for 10 minutes. Reduce the heat and simmer until the vegetables are tender. Add more water if needed. Serves 16.

This is my "lose weight during the winter months blahs" soup. Not only does it warm you up but you feel good about getting your servings of veggies. This soup can be eaten as the main meal or as a smaller bowl before the main meal to curb your appetite. Here's to happy eating and kissing those extra pounds good-bye!

Debbie Greene Moxley

Easy Crock-Pot Soup

1 pound ground beef
1 medium onion, diced
Two 14-ounce cans beef broth
2 cups water
15-ounce can sweet peas, drained
14½-ounce can cut green beans, drained
15¼-ounce can whole kernel corn, drained
15-ounce can sliced potatoes, drained
14½-ounce can sliced carrots, drained
14½-ounce can diced tomatoes, drained
Salt and pepper to taste

Brown the ground beef and onion in a large skillet; drain. Place
the beef and onion in a Crock-Pot. Add the remaining ingredients
and mix. Cook on high for 2 hours or on low for 4 to 6 hours.

Angela Young

Sandy's Green Chili Stew

2 pounds stew meat, cut into small pieces
3 cups frozen or canned corn
3 stalks celery, diced
3 medium potatoes, peeled and diced
5 green chili peppers, roasted and diced
3 cups water

Brown the meat in a large pot. Add the remaining ingredients.
Cover and simmer for approximately 1 hour, stirring occasionally.

Sandy Back

Gene's Chili Roll Chili

1½ pounds ground beef
1 medium onion, chopped
1 pound chili roll
2 cups water
2 cups tomato juice
½ cup ketchup
15½-ounce can chili beans
1 tablespoon chili powder
1 teaspoon salt
¼ teaspoon black pepper
¼ teaspoon seasoned salt

Brown the ground beef and onion in a skillet; drain. Place in a
large saucepan. Add the remaining ingredients. Bring to a boil,
stirring occasionally. Reduce the heat and simmer for about 15
minutes stirring occasionally. Serves 8.

Emogene Miller Moseley

Stripping Tobacco, a Family Affair

For 29 years Dennis and I spent the summer and fall months growing and harvesting tobacco and the winter months stripping tobacco. I worked alongside my mother-in-law, Ruby Ralph, and father-in-law, Andrew Ralph, for several years and also my mom and dad, Emogene and Charles Moseley. The first time I stripped tobacco for Andrew and Ruby was in 1978. We worked in an open barn at Uncle Charles Ralph's home place. Our only source of heat was a small fire in the middle of the barn. The doorway was covered with plastic to keep the heat in and the frigid cold wind out. For lunch, Ruby brought along her big cast-iron skillet to fry up eggs and homemade sausages, a kettle for boiling coffee water and a Claxton Fruit Cake left over from Christmas. The fireside was warm and the camp style cooking was great.

Stripping tobacco on Dad's farm included the conveniences of an enclosed stripping room, electricity and a kerosene heater, but we couldn't totally escape the chill of winter. I often took the children to the tobacco barn, especially the two boys, Andy and Robert, after Julie entered kindergarten. She had asthma and the tobacco dust made her ill. Mom always brought food for our lunch. She arose early in the morning to pack sandwich meat, bread, crackers and a pot of chili. She heated the chili in a crock-pot before lunchtime. Our family looked forward to eating her chili. It warms my heart today to know that Mom has always taken the time to make every occasion with family special.

Judith Ralph

Hot Tamale Chili

2½ pounds ground beef
4 quarts homemade tomato juice
Two 1¼-ounce packages chili seasoning
½ pound spaghetti noodles
Dash of chili powder
Dash of cayenne pepper

Brown the ground beef in a large pot; drain. Add the remaining ingredients and cook until the noodles are done.

This is mine and Junior's special chili recipe. Last fall several of us got together up on the hill and wanted to fix something to eat. I wanted to cook a simple meal without a lot of different dishes. Junior and I started mixing together different ingredients to make a big pot of chili and it was good. We fed about 20 people that day.

Brenda Ambrose

Minestrone Soup

3 tablespoons olive oil
3 zucchini, washed and cut into quarter slices with peeling
2 cups sliced celery
1 medium onion, diced
3 cloves garlic, peeled and mashed
14½-ounce can diced tomatoes
16-ounce can kidney beans, drained
15-ounce can garbanzo beans, drained
1 cup rice, cooked
3 carrots, peeled and sliced thin
2 tablespoons basil
1 tablespoon oregano
1 teaspoon rosemary
6 cups beef broth

Heat the olive oil in a skillet over a medium heat. Sauté the zucchini, celery, onion and garlic until the vegetables start to soften. Place the sautéed vegetables and the remaining ingredients in a soup pot. Cook over a medium heat for 1 hour.

After eating a bowl of Minestrone soup at the Olive Garden I wanted to recreate the dish at home. This is my perfected recipe after mixing and cooking the ingredients a couple of times. It is quite yummy.

Debbie Tron

Seven Can Soup

10¾-ounce can tomato soup
10¾-ounce can vegetable soup
15-ounce can chili with beans
15-ounce can chili without beans
15¼-ounce can whole kernel corn, undrained
15-ounce can mixed vegetables, undrained
14½-ounce can diced tomatoes
1 pound ground beef, cooked and drained

Combine all of the ingredients in a large soup pan. Simmer until thoroughly heated. This is a very tasty and filling dish to make, not to mention it is quick and easy.

Carol Estes

HAMBURGER FRY WITH THE BROWND FAMILY

When my dad was a child, his mother fixed cheeseburgers and fried potatoes every Saturday night for supper. Now my mom makes cheeseburgers and fried potatoes for supper on Saturday nights and my family and I go over to eat. My mom wants me to carry on the tradition once she is no longer able to continue, and I definitely plan on it.

Gretchen Jones

The Famous Doris Ann Cambron Burgoo

3 pound beef roast
4 pound baked hen
3 pounds mutton
½ pound navy beans, cooked without seasoning
1 gallon tomatoes, diced
1½ heads cabbage, diced
3 pounds onion, diced
7 pounds potatoes, diced
1 gallon tomato juice
½ gallon water
¼ cup lemon juice
¼ cup cider vinegar
½ cup sugar
½ cup Worcestershire sauce
Salt and pepper to taste
6 pints whole kernel corn

Place the beef roast in a roasting pan and cover with water; cook until done. Separate the fat and bone from the meat. Grind the meat through a ¼-inch plate. Discard the scraps and save the broth.

Place the baking hen in a roasting pan and cover with water; cook until done. Separate the fat and bone from the meat. Grind the meat through a ¼-inch plate. Discard the scraps and save the broth.

Place the mutton in a roasting pan and cover with water; cook until done. Separate the fat and bone from the meat. Grind the meat through a ¼-inch plate. Discard the scraps and the broth.

Cook the beans according to the package directions. Combine the beans, tomatoes, cabbage, onions, potatoes, roast, hen, mutton, reserved broth and water in a 10-gallon pot; stir. Cook over a medium-high heat for 1 hour. Add the lemon juice, vinegar, sugar and Worcestershire sauce and stir. Add the salt and pepper. Cook for 30 to 40 minutes. Add the corn and cook for 1 hour and 15 minutes or until the vegetables are done. Stir every 15 minutes, adding water as needed. Makes approximately 6 gallons.

This recipe started when Ann Cambron, of German descent, was cooking 20 gallons of vegetable soup with some friends on the banks of the Ohio River. Ann had made Burgoo before but this vegetable soup recipe was more to her liking. She decided to alter the recipe by changing the mixed vegetables and so it became The Famous Doris Ann Cambron Burgoo.

Norman Cambron

Adrian Adair Richards

When our great-granddaughter Adrian was small she spent the majority of her time at our house. With the exception of my job at the paper mill, I ignored my projects and devoted my time to playing with her. We rode the three-wheeler, played with dolls and horses under the bed, and watched the Lion King at least 300 times. She quickly became the best buddy I had ever had and I became the person she called for anytime she needed something. I valued our time together, but I didn't realize how much she valued our time until we had the following conversation on the phone one night.

Adrian had gone on vacation with us starting when she was a little over one year old. She always looked forward to and was excited about going after she was old enough to understand. She wanted to go to the beach so that's where we always went. At this time we were planning a trip to Florida, Adrian was a couple months shy of four years old.

She called one night as she often did and after the usual chit chat, she asked if I had to work the next day. She always fussed at me for having to go to work instead of playing with her. I answered that I did have to go to work and she asked why. I told her that I had to work to make some money. She answered, "you've got some money, I saw it, you've got lotsa quarters," referring to the change bowl that I kept in my drawer. So trying to give her a good reason, I told her that it costs a lot of money to go on vacation, and that I had to work so we could go on vacation. I was not prepared for the answer that I got when after a short silence she said, "I don't want to go on vacation." I was honored that a little girl thought that much of me.

Leonard C. Adkins

Salads

Back row: Louella Alma Stinnett Moseley, Esther Moseley, John Moseley.
Front row: George (Red) Moseley, Charles Moseley.

Great-grandma Alma Moseley purchased one of the first two pianos to be shipped down the Ohio River. Dad remembers her "banging" on that piano at family gatherings on the home place, one song in particular, Home on the Range. She never used sheet music.

Judith Ralph

In Memory of My Loving Mother, Nila Back

I spend a lot of time thinking about my life and my years growing up. People often talk about the good old days and how things were simple but so much better.

My mother lived a simple life but things sure weren't better for her. Her life was never easy. She worked so hard in the fields in the hot sun, then cooked, washed clothes on a wash board and hung them on a line in the winter and the summer. I have seen the clothes freeze stiff on the clothesline. Mother drew water from the well and heated it in an iron kettle over an open fire. She always managed to have a hot meal on the table by the time we got home from school. Besides having all of us to cook for, she had a lot of visiting relatives and she always cooked the best she had and worried that it might not be good enough. The only things us kids worried about was not getting to eat at the table until the grown ups were finished. They sure took their time about leaving the table. If mom was glad when the relatives left, she never said so.

Mom always said the happiest times of her life were when all ten (10) of us kids were home. Well, the happiest times of my life were when I was able to be with my mother. There may come a time when I may not be able to remember my mother and all she has done for us children but I know one thing for sure, she will always be in my heart.

Kathryn Bailey

Bonnie's Tuna Salad

6-ounce can chunk light tuna, drained
2 hard-boiled eggs, diced
3 sweet pickles, diced
3 tablespoons salad dressing

Combine all of the ingredients in a bowl. Cover and chill. Good on bread, crackers, a bed of lettuce or just by itself.

My neighbor Bonnie used to make tuna salad for our snack. It was my favorite at her house. She wrote it on a recipe card at my wedding shower, 27 years ago and I still have it!

Shelia Oliver Thurman

FRIENDS FOR LIFE

When I was 3 years old I made a best friend for life, Cheryl Richards, now Harden. Now we are grown and have busy lives and families of our own. But when we get together it's like we've never been apart. Cheryl's mother, Bonnie became my other mother. When we went on car trips to town Bonnie would always sing and we would sing too. Bonnie once made Cheryl and me little yellow tops just alike and we pretended to be real sisters. Bonnie let us mess up her house with Barbie dolls and dress up clothes. We loved to collect boxes of rocks and fossils. We would draw pictures on paper with chalk. And, of all things decided to "develop" them in water in the basement bathroom and let them dry on the wall. My childhood was enriched by those two ladies and I will always treasure those memories.

Shelia Oliver Thurman

Carol Ann's Pasta Salad

½ pound pasta, any kind
1 green pepper, finely chopped
1 cucumber, finely chopped
1 large ripe tomato, chopped
1 green onion stem, finely chopped
1 stalk celery, finely chopped
½ 10-ounce box frozen peas, cooked and drained
16-ounce bottle buttermilk dressing

Cook the pasta according to the package directions and drain well.
Combine all of the ingredients to moisten. Add more of the
dressing when ready to serve. Store, covered, in the refrigerator.
Add bacon bits, cheese, or paprika for variety. The amounts used
are optional as to the number of people.

Carol Ann Robbins

Randy's Spaghetti Salad

1 pound spaghetti
8 ounces Italian salad dressing
1 large ripe tomato, chopped
1 large red bell pepper, chopped
1 large green bell pepper, chopped
1 large cucumber, peeled and chopped
1 medium onion, peeled and chopped
Salt and pepper to taste

Cook the spaghetti according to the package directions. Combine
all of the ingredients in a serving bowl. Chill until ready to serve.

Randy Back

Frozen Cranberry Salad

1 cup whole-berry cranberry sauce
20-ounce can crushed pineapples, drained
1 cup chopped pecans
8-ounce carton prepared whipped topping
10¾-ounce can sweetened condensed milk

Combine all of the ingredients in an 8x8-inch freezer-safe container. Freeze overnight. Allow the frozen salad to thaw for approximately 15 minutes. Slice into serving size pieces. Makes 10 to 12 servings.

My mother-in-law is a most remarkable lady. She was left a widow to raise 5 children, the youngest, my husband Ralph, was 2 at the time. Kathryn worked as many as 3 jobs at a time. She would leave her school cafeteria job to clean offices. At night she would sit with the elderly. Through all of this Kathryn never asked for government assistance. She had her own medical remedies that she would use. I remember one time being at her kitchen sink and her making a comment, "a woman just can't make it without a man." I never said anything but I immediately thought, "what does she think she's been doing all these years?" She has managed very well.

Kim Mitchell

Kathryn
and Ricky

Granny Porter's Turkey Salad

3 cups cooked and chopped cold turkey
1½ cups chopped celery
½ small onion, minced
1 cup chopped pickles
1 cup mayonnaise
4 hard-boiled eggs, chopped
1 tablespoon chopped green or red bell pepper
1 tablespoon vinegar
1 tablespoon salt and pepper

Combine all of the ingredients in a bowl. Refrigerate until ready to serve. Serve as a sandwich or as a salad on crisp lettuce or other greens. Serves 16 (1½ cup serving size).

My mom, Margaret Allen, used to make this for me after Thanksgiving because that was the only time we had leftover turkey. It's the best and I always loved it.

Heather Litsey

Lime Gelatin Salad

½ cup sugar
Two 6-ounce boxes lime gelatin
2 cups miniature marshmallows
2 cups hot water
2 cups crushed pineapple, drained
Two 8-ounce packages cream cheese, at room temperature
2 cups prepared whipped topping
2 cups chopped pecans

Combine the sugar, gelatin and marshmallows in a large bowl.
Pour the water over the mixture and stir until dissolved.
Refrigerate until slightly thickened. Combine the crushed
pineapple and cream cheese in a separate bowl and beat well.
Add to the gelatin mixture and beat well. Fold in the whipped
topping and nuts.

*Christmas is a time we look forward to because our favorite foods are often
prepared only at this time. My mother made a green gelatin salad each year that
became a favorite of mine. I liked to think she made it just for me, since I was the
one who would come home from the greatest distance.*

Brenda Young

BELLS OF CHRISTMAS

*Mamaw Miller used to stand out on the sun porch with me and listen
to the Christmas chimes ring at Fordsville Baptist Church. The wind
made the porch really cold.*

Barry Moseley

Nancy's Layered Hot Potato Salad

8 medium whole red potatoes, sliced with peelings
8 hard-boiled eggs, peeled and sliced
1 medium onion, chopped
1 pound bacon, fried and crumbled
2 cups salad dressing
6 tablespoons mustard
½ cup sugar

Cover the bottom of a 10½ x 14¾-inch baking dish with the sliced potatoes. Layer the eggs, onion and bacon. Combine the salad dressing, mustard and sugar in a bowl and pour over the top. Bake at 350 degrees for 30 minutes or until the potatoes are tender.

Tamara Taylor

TORMENT

I remember like it was yesterday when I was a little girl playing around in the kitchen while Mama was cooking. When I burned my finger on the stove I would complain and complain. Mama would always say, "Now Lorene, remember how bad that finger hurts. When you grow up if you are not a good girl and don't accept Jesus as your Savior you will go to a bad place where you will burn forever." She always called that bad place torment and I knew that was one place that I did not want to go.

Lorene Leach Wright

Pistachio Salad

3.4-ounce box pistachio instant pudding
8-ounce can crushed pineapple, undrained
11-ounce can mandarin oranges, drained
1 cup miniature marshmallows
12-ounce container whipped topping
½ cup halved maraschino cherries

Dissolve the pudding in the pineapple. Add the remaining
ingredients except the cherries; mix well. Spoon the mixture into
a medium decorative bowl. Garnish with the cherries. The dish
keeps well for several days in the refrigerator.

*Family meals, a table of communication. When we gather our families around our
tables for a holiday meal, we always begin with a blessing and then our meal. This
is a tradition that began with Mama. The meal would always include many of her
recipes. Pistachio salad was one of my favorites. Mama passed away in January
1997. Her holiday traditions continue. The recipes are precious memories for my
sister, Carol, and me.*

                                                      Dee Dee Ransdall

Red Potato Salad

10 medium potatoes, skin on
1 small onion, chopped
7 strips bacon, cooked and crumbled
1 stalk celery, chopped
1 tablespoon spicy mustard
Salt to taste
Pepper to taste
Parsley flakes to taste
Salad dressing to taste
1 tablespoon dry ranch dressing mix
Paprika

Cook the potatoes in boiling water until tender; cool. Cut the potatoes into small cubes. Combine the potatoes, onion, bacon, celery, mustard, salt, pepper, parsley flakes and salad dressing in a bowl; stir well. Add the ranch dressing mix and stir. Top with the paprika and chill for 2 hours before serving.

Melinda Schneider

Those Few Short Words

One of the best discipline tools mom used with us was just a few short words. Anytime we were leaving the house she would call after us, "Don't do anything you wouldn't want to be doing if Jesus came back." I must say that ran through my mind many times and many times I've said, "Lord, get me out of this situation and I won't do it again."

Kim Mitchell

Strawberry Spinach Salad

9 cups torn fresh spinach
1 pint fresh strawberries, capped and halved
½ cup slivered almonds, toasted

Dressing

¼ cup vegetable oil
2 tablespoons sugar
2 tablespoons cider vinegar
1 tablespoon chopped onion
1 teaspoon poppy seeds
¼ teaspoon paprika
⅛ teaspoon Worcestershire sauce

Combine the spinach, strawberries and almonds in a large bowl.
Combine the dressing ingredients in a blender container; cover and
process until combined. Pour over the salad and toss to coat.
Serve immediately.

Kim Mitchell

*We are all so blessed to have a wonderful family and the privilege to get together
when we can.*

Kathryn Bailey

Ruby Ralph
November 9, 1927 to present

I worship the ground that my Mama walks on. She was one tough woman. She had a heart of steel and she had a heart of gold... She worked that farm... She took care of us kids... She washed our clothes...She fixed our meals...She fed all six of us kids... She stayed up 'til 3:00 in the morning canning... She had a hot meal waiting for us at 5:00 am.

My Mama taught me everything. She taught me how to love, how to give, how to cook, how to clean, how to treat people, and how to take up for myself. That is the main thing that my Mama taught me. We sat at the kitchen table a lot of times, Mama would say, "Don't you let no man run over you." She told me that a thousand times. I told Mama that no man is going to run over me. I promised her that.

She told me to go out and find you a good man, a man that will love you and will treat you right. And I did. He has given me two wonderful kids. And now I have two wonderful grandkids, thanks to my Mama.

Connie Ralph Boling

Main Dishes

Our Wedding Day, October 1, 1976
Dennis and Judith Ralph with Mamaw Agnes Miles, Great-grandmother Leach
and Papaw Clarence Miller

Dad says that Mom knew how to cook from day one. Dennis says that he taught me how to cook. Maybe so! He actually remembers the first meal that I prepared for him as a new bride...fried pork chops, fried potatoes, and barbecued beans.

Judith Ralph

Sudi Oliver

I was my great grandmother Sudie's first great grandchild, and my memories date back to her when I was six years old. She was in her 80's when she had a stroke. I remember her lying in a bed, and I was told she had not spoken for two months. Out of my love for her, I would peek around the door opening to see her. My mother would caution me not to disturb her. Finally, my need to be close to her overcame my instructions to remain at bay. I approached her bedside only to hear her say my name, with delight. Then she began to sing a lullaby that she had sung to me many times before. The song went:

Mama's gonna buy you a mocking bird, when that mockingbird don't sing, Mama's gonna buy you a diamond ring, when that diamond ring turns to brass, Mama's gonna buy you a looking glass...

I can't remember the rest of the words, but I remember after she had sung the song, she passed away. I was too young to understand she had died and I asked why my grandmother put coins on her eyelids, and covered her with a sheet?

Sudi was always the one who would go out to the road to meet mourners in her day, when the family with a loved one, in a casket on the back of a road wagon, approached. She would send for the best ham out of the smoke house to cook a meal for the mourners. She offered her place for a time of rest before the family proceeded to the burial place. She was a very respected and loved person in the community. I still have her wedding band that I received on the day of her death.

Brenda Oliver Young

Chicken Casserole

3 or 4 cooked chicken breasts, deboned and cubed
10½-ounce can cream of mushroom condensed soup
10½-ounce can cream of celery condensed soup
1½ cups milk
6-ounce box stuffing mix

Combine the chicken, soups and milk in a 3-quart baking dish. Prepare the stuffing according to the package directions. Top the casserole with the stuffing. Cover with aluminum foil and bake at 350 degrees for 20 minutes. Uncover and let brown.

When I was a young child Mama always cooked a big meal and the leftovers were kept in the middle of the table with a tablecloth covering them. Mama placed an *oil cloth on the surface of the table and the tablecloth covering the food was usually made of feed sack cloth. Its purpose was to keep flies away from the food. This also made it less tempting for us to nibble between meals. Beneath this tablecloth Mama also kept a small can of Pet milk used for coffee creamer. I often sneaked sips from the can when no one was watching.

Jerl Dean Adkins

*Oil cloth was sold in general stores by the foot from large paper rolls. It is a type of cloth made waterproof by a coating of paint or treatment of oil.

Chicken 'N Dumplings

1 baking hen
Three to four 14½-ounce cans chicken broth
3 tablespoons butter
3 cups sifted all-purpose flour
4 teaspoons baking powder
1½ teaspoons salt
1½ cups milk
Pepper to taste

Bake the hen according to the package directions; cool. Pick the meat off of the bones and reserve the broth. Heat the reserved broth and the canned broth in a large pot. Bring to a boil.

Cut the butter into the flour in a bowl. Add the remaining ingredients and mix well. Roll the dough to ⅛ inch thickness on a floured board. Cut into squares. Drop the squares, one at a time, in the boiling broth and boil for 15 minutes. Add the chicken and pepper. Use more canned broth if needed.

My Mom, Betty Tinney, has always been an excellent cook, rarely using a boxed mix. Her meals are made from scratch, with hard working hands that are always busy in the kitchen. There is nothing that pleases Mom more than seeing others enjoy her mealtime spread. We all have our favorites. Going to Mom's for a holiday always makes the palate water, in waiting for the variety of her delicious dishes. Her kids and grandkids always await her big pot of homemade chicken and dumplings. I decided after Mom had her first heart attack that if I wished to enjoy the same dishes when she is gone, I better get recipes, ask questions and learn to make them myself. I have learned to make several of them and have passed the dumpling recipe on to my daughter, Jesalyn. She has helped me a time or two with them. However, her HELP right now, as she is 11 years old, is drawing me hearts in the flour. That's OK by me, at least we are getting quality time together and she is learning little bits at a time. Years down the road I am hoping Jesalyn's family will have the pleasure of tasting this handed-down family recipe. In turn she will reminisce eating them at Granny's and making them with Mom.

Becky Pfaff

Chicken Nibby

Chicken breast tenders, uncooked
Sour cream
Cheese flavored crackers, crushed
Margarine, melted
Salt and pepper to taste

Roll the chicken tenders in the sour cream and then into the crushed crackers. Place the tenders in a 9x13-inch baking dish. Sprinkle the melted margarine over the top. Add the salt and pepper. Bake at 350 degrees for about 20 minutes or until done. I have never really timed them. I just watch them.

This is a recipe that I used in college. I lived in a Christian ministry house with up to 5 other girls. Being poor college students, we would pool our money and buy the ingredients to make this a couple of times each month. We would make 2 and 3 pans at a time. I think the best part of it was the assembly line preparation and most of all...the girl talk while cooking/eating.

Angela Young

Mrs. Leach wrapped left over fried chicken in aluminum foil to refrigerate. When she removed it to reheat, she opened the foil, placed it in an iron skillet on top of the stove and heated. It was as good as or better than the day she first fried it.

Joyce Leach

Chicken Pot Pie

Two 10¾-ounce cans cream of potato soup
15-ounce can mixed vegetables, drained
1½ cups diced cooked chicken
½ cup milk
½ teaspoon pepper
Two 9-inch pie crusts, unbaked
1 egg, slightly beaten

Combine the first 5 ingredients.   Place on of the the pie crusts in the bottom of a pie pan. Spoon the mixture into the crust. Cover with the remaining crust crimping the edges to seal. Slit the top crust and brush with the egg. Bake at 375 degrees for 40 minutes. Cool for 10 minutes before serving.

My mom, Kellie Ralph, cooks the best chicken pot pie I have ever tasted. I can speak for a lot of people. I say that her cooking is good especially when she cooks chicken pot pie.

Tyler McManaway

Non-traditional

When my youngest son, Robert, married, I was fortunate to inherit two fine young men, Nicholas and Tyler McManaway as grandsons. Their mother, Kellie, planned a non-traditional wedding ceremony choosing her two sons to be the "maid of honor and the bridesmaid." We joked about the idea but in all actuality it warmed my heart that she chose to include her boys, symbolically uniting the family and the couple.

Judith Ralph

Cowboy Beans

1 pound lean ground beef
½ cup chopped onion
¼ cup ketchup
¼ cup barbecue sauce
¼ cup granulated sugar
¼ cup brown sugar
2 tablespoons sorghum or other molasses
1 tablespoon chili powder
1 teaspoon salt
1 teaspoon pepper
2 tablespoons prepared yellow mustard
16-ounce can pork 'n beans
16-ounce can butter beans, drained
16-ounce can kidney beans, drained
16-ounce can pinto beans, drained
½ pound bacon, cooked and crumbles

Brown the ground beef and onion and cook until the onion is tender; drain well. Add the remaining ingredients except the bacon. Place the mixture in a 9x13-inch baking dish or crock-pot and top with bacon crumbs. Bake at 350 degrees for 1 hour or cook in the crock-pot on HIGH for 1 hour. Reduce the heat and cook for 2 to 4 hours on LOW.

Kim Mitchell

WOW: If you are self-taught, you really want to learn.
Bill Spradling

Granny's Stuffed Hot Dogs

2 cups mashed potatoes
½ cup finely chopped onions, optional
1 pound package hot dogs
Mustard, optional
4 cheese slices or 1 cup shredded

Combine the mashed potatoes and onion. Slice each hot dog like
a hot dog bun, being careful not to cut through. Put a stripe of
mustard in the middle of each hot dog. Fill each hot dog with the
potato mixture. Top with the cheese. Place the hot dogs on a
baking sheet. Bake at 350 degrees for 15 minutes or until the
cheese is melted and starts to bubble.

*This is great for using left over mashed potatoes. Most kids like hot dogs and
mashed potatoes, why not put them together! My grandmother made this for me
as a child. All my friends thought it was disgusting until they tried it! You can
vary the amounts for your taste and/or how many people you are feeding.
Serves 5 to 10.*

Angela Young

No Knob Stove

*I remember sitting in that old, white painted high chair at Mamaw
Miller's house eating a boiled hot dog and watching her cook. My
back was against the door. She would be working around the kitchen
with a scarf tied around her head. She looked sort of like Aunt
Jemima. Her stove had some of the knobs missing and she would
have to take a pair of pliers to turn on the burners. I would wonder
why didn't she buy a new stove.*

Barry Moseley

Honey Brine Turkey

1 gallon hot water
1 pound kosher salt
16 ounces honey
2 quarts vegetable broth
7-pound bag ice
15 to 20-pound turkey, giblets removed

Combine the hot water, salt and honey in a 54-quart cooler. Stir until the salt and honey are dissolved. Add the vegetable broth and ice and stir. Place the turkey in the brine, breast side up. Add water until the turkey is almost covered. Close the cooler lid and let set up to 12 hours or over night. Remove the turkey from the brine and drain thoroughly. Cook as you would normally.

Andrew Hollifield

For the past several years, our local Family Resource Centers have offered a cooking class to our community families. The main reason for the class is to teach families how to properly thaw and cook a turkey. This past year Andrew prepared the turkey that we used for class demonstration with the recipe above. It was wonderful!

Kim Mitchell

> WOW: A very dear pastor's wife once told me, "Say it once and you're concerned. Say it twice and you're a nag."

Hot Chicken Salad

2 pounds boneless chicken breast
4 cups diced celery
10½-ounce can cream of chicken soup
2 cups mayonnaise
2 cups sour cream
Two 8-ounce cans diced water chestnuts, drained
8-ounce jar sliced mushrooms, drained
1 cup slivered almonds
2 tablespoons chopped onion
2 tablespoons lemon juice
2 teaspoons salt
½ teaspoon pepper
2 cups shredded Cheddar cheese
Two 8-ounce cans French-fried onions

Cook the chicken in water in a saucepan; drain. Cut the chicken
into bite-size pieces. Place in a 9x13-inch baking dish Add the
remaining ingredients except the cheese and French-fried onions;
stir. Sprinkle the cheese over the top. Bake at 350 degrees for
20 minutes. Add the French-fried onions and bake an additional
10 minutes.

Stacey Webb

*I went from the age of the horse and buggy, to the age of the automobile to the age
of rockets. That is a lot of change in the lifetime of one person.*

Bill Spradling

Keni's Hamburger Stew

¾ cup ground beef
5 to 6 potatoes, peeled and diced
1 medium onion, chopped
10¾-ounce can tomato soup
2 soup cans water or enough to cover
2 teaspoons chili powder
Salt and pepper to taste

Brown the ground beef in a large, heavy saucepan. Add the potatoes, onions, tomato soup, water, chili powder, salt and pepper. Cook for about 30 to 40 minutes or until tender. Serve over buttered bread.

Hamburger Stew has been a staple in our family for years. I was born in Cincinnati, OH and lived there, off and on until I was 12. A lady lived across the street who was a widow and had raised 6 kids. She really had to stretch things to make ends meet and this recipe is one she used about twice a week. She gave it to my mom, Maxine Halsey, and it has been a favorite of the family since then. We've always kidded that if you have unexpected guests show up for dinner you only have to throw in another "tater." Serve with bread, butter and a dish of coleslaw and you have a filling meal.

Keni Spradling

No Peek Pot Roast

3 to 4-pound pot roast, frozen
1 medium onion, chopped
1-ounce package onion soup mix
4-ounce can sliced mushrooms
Salt and pepper to taste
Dash of garlic powder
2.64-ounce package brown gravy mix

Place the frozen roast in a 4-quart glass baking dish. Add the remaining ingredients; mix well. Add enough water to fill ½ full. Cover and bake at 275 degrees for 2 hours. Turn the temperature up to 350 degrees and bake for 1 hour. Do not open oven until time is up.

My best friend, Sharon Sharp, gave me this recipe. She always made the best pot roasts. They were tender and tasted great. She has died since then, but I am sure if there is cooking in Heaven she's right there at a big stove making some really tasty food for all those heavenly angels.

Cindy Burns

Pizza Casserole

1 pound ground chuck
1 teaspoon salt
½ teaspoon pepper
26-ounce jar spaghetti sauce
16-ounce box spaghetti noodles
3½-ounce package sliced pepperoni
2 cups shredded mozzarella cheese
1 cup shredded Cheddar cheese

Brown the ground chuck in a skillet. Season with the salt and pepper; drain. Add the spaghetti sauce and cook over a low heat for 10 minutes. Cook the noodles according to the package directions; drain. Add the noodles to the meat mixture and mix well. Place ½ the spaghetti in the bottom of a 9x13-inch glass dish. Add ½ of the pepperonis. Top with 1 cup of the mozzarella cheese and ½ cup of the Cheddar cheese. Repeat with the remaining ingredients. Bake, covered, at 425 degrees for about 25 minutes. Uncover and bake an additional 5 minutes or until the cheese starts to brown.

My mom and my mamaw are the two most important and influential women in my life. They are both dedicated to our family. I am thankful to have so many fond memories of the special times that we have had together as a family.

Julie Ralph Alford

Taco Casserole

3 pounds ground chuck
Three 1¼-ounce packages taco seasoning
2½ cups water
Eight 8-inch flour tortillas
15-ounce can chili without beans
8-ounce package fiesta blend shredded cheese

Cook the ground chuck in a large skillet and drain. Add the taco seasoning and water and simmer over a medium heat, stirring occasionally, until thickened. Line the bottom and sides of a 4-quart glass casserole dish with 4 of the tortillas and fill with ½ of the meat mixture. Repeat layering with 2 tortillas, the remaining meat mixture and the remaining 2 tortillas. Spread the chili on the top and sprinkle with the cheese. Bake, uncovered, at 350 degrees for about 5 minutes or until the cheese is melted. Serve with taco sauce.

This casserole is one of the many dishes that I left on the stovetop for my sons and their friends when coming in from a late night out. The kitchen door was always open.

Judith Ralph

WOW: Family members are the foundation blocks upon which a home is built. God is the mortar that holds them in place. It's the Kentucky way.

Judith Ralph

Salmon Patties

¼ cup chopped green peppers
¼ cup chopped onion
2 eggs, beaten
¾ sleeve saltine crackers
16-ounce can salmon, drained

Combine all of the ingredients in a bowl. Pat into 4 patties. Fry in a vegetable oil/bacon grease mixture, as this gives a little flavor. Fry until brown on each side. I thicken a can of peas and use as a topping for the patties.

Carol Ann Robbins

CHRISTMAS TRADITION

Every Christmas our family has gathered on Christmas Eve to celebrate Christmas. The very first thing we do is gather around and read the Christmas story. Dad began this tradition before any of us could read. He usually read out of Luke chapter 2. As we got older, one of us children would read, thinking we could possibly read it a little faster than dad. My first Christmas away from the family was during my first pregnancy. I was too far along to travel. That particular Christmas Eve evening I called home about the time I knew everyone would be gathering together and had dad read the story over the phone...that was the last Christmas we would miss that tradition. Many grandchildren have been added since then and now they take turns reading the Christmas story. After the story is read, we then pray together, and finally open our gifts.

Kim Mitchell

Slow Cooker Cranberry Pork
Roast

3 to 4-pound boneless pork loin roast, halved
2 tablespoons vegetable oil
16-ounce can whole-berry cranberry sauce
¾ cup sugar
¾ cup cranberry juice
1 teaspoon ground mustard
1 teaspoon pepper
¼ teaspoon ground cloves

Gravy

¼ cup cornstarch
¼ cup cold water
Salt and pepper to taste

Brown the roast on all sides in the oil in a Dutch oven over a medium-high heat. Transfer the roast to a 5-quart slow cooker. Combine the cranberry sauce, sugar, cranberry juice, mustard, pepper and cloves in a bowl; pour over the roast. Cover and cook on low for 6 to 8 hours or until the meat thermometer reads 160 degrees. Remove the roast and keep warm.

Combine the cornstarch, water, salt and pepper in a saucepan. Stir in the cooking juices from the roast. Bring to a boil and cook for 2 minutes or until thickened, stirring constantly. Serve with the roast.

Myrl Ralph

Tuna Croquettes

1 tablespoon shortening
1 tablespoon self-rising flour
½ cup milk
6-ounce can spring water tuna, drained
Salt and pepper to taste
2 eggs, beaten
10 cups white bread, broken into pieces

Combine the shortening, flour and milk in a skillet and heat until it thickens. Set aside to cool. Add the tuna, salt and pepper and mix well. Drop the mixture by teaspoonfuls into the egg. Roll the mixture in the bread pieces. Deep fry until golden brown. Makes 20.

I got this recipe from Ethel Boling my grandmother-in-law. She had this cookbook that was made from an old school book. She saved her Mother's Day cards and birthday cards and glued them onto the pages of the book next to the sender's favorite recipe. The pages also contained other recipes she had clipped and saved. It was a great idea.

When we moved on the farm that we got from Ethel and Randolph I would make this tuna croquette recipe and take to them. Randolph would ask where did I learn to make these and I would say "your wife taught me this."

The croquettes go great with pinto beans and boiled potatoes.

Debra Taylor

THE LETTER

My dear mother is watching each day
For a letter still not on its way
And her heart is sinking in despair,
Believing that I no longer care.

I love her more than she will ever know
And am glad I have often told her so:
But so many things keep coming my way
That I wait to write her some other day.

I am much too busy, it seems,
For my heart is full of dreams;
But I suppose it will always be that way,
So I am going to write that letter today!

The Late Myrtle Marie Leach Mayer

My great-aunt wrote this poem and numerous others. She often dreamed of becoming a published poet. Not having had children, I am sure she spent countless hours pondering the simplicities of life that we so often take for granted. From within her heart she honestly conveyed her deepest emotions-from those of sorrow and loneliness to those of joy and contentment.

Judith Ralph

Memories and Keepsakes

I am from a small country town, a circle of family, good books, stories passed on, a loving place called home and my parent's prayers.

I am from the garden in the fresh springtime where young plants with tender necks were placed gently in the soil with all the hope of things to come.

I am from fuchsia and crimson Hollyhocks, Morning Glories trailing on a string, and Bleeding Hearts in soft colors of pink and white in my Grandmother's garden. Now they are always on my own.
I am from southern cooking, overstuffed feather beds, and sweet smelling Lavender.

I am the gift of Buddy and Tinker Bell. Daddy's girl! Don't give up! Be brave! We love you!
I am from the worn, tattered family Bible where Grandma wrote down joyful births and sorrowful deaths, a white clapboard church were "Amazing Grace" and the "Old Rugged Cross" were sung in sweet harmony on Sunday mornings.

I am from Grandpa's rugged hands folding in prayer over our Sunday dinner of fried chicken, homemade biscuits and fresh apple pie.
I am from tractor rides with my grandpa on warm sunny days, blackberry picking, scratching chiggers and eating red tomatoes fresh from the vine.

I am from gentle cows in the pasture that come to the sound of my Daddy's call. Stray, shaggy dogs that needed a home. Cats that had kittens hidden in the barn while my eager cousins and I hunted for them.

Memories and keepsakes are forever embedded in my essence. All that I am or hope to become are because of where I have been from those who have loved me. My one hope, my final ambition is to pass on to my daughter the love and laughter I have known. May I use these gifts that I have been given to create a new gift. My Daughter!

Vickey Fulkerson

SIDE DISHES

December 1962
Charles and Emogene Moseley, Judith and Barry

In earlier years, Mom enjoyed preparing family dinners and setting the dining room table with her best china, crystal and linens. Once we had fresh corn on the cob I was small and could barely reach the table. After taking a sip from the crystal goblet I was horrified at the buttery fingerprints plastered all over the glass.

Judith Ralph

Cheese Sauce for Cauliflower

2 tablespoons margarine
2 tablespoons self-rising flour
1 tablespoon dry mustard
¼ teaspoon salt
¼ teaspoon pepper
1 cup milk
1 cup American cheese
5 drops hot sauce

Melt the margarine in a skillet over a low heat. Add the flour, mustard, salt and pepper and stir constantly. Blend in the milk, continuing to stir until it boils and thickens. Add the cheese and hot sauce, stirring until the cheese is melted. Pour over cooked cauliflower.

To Emogene Moseley
1993

Mamaw,
It is great to have a Mamaw because she is always there for us when we are sick and she is always looking forward for us to visit.

Love You
4-ever
and
always
Andrew
Ralph

I really look forward to this Sunday dinner dish of my mother's. Mom has a way of preparing foods that are so tasty and unique you just can't go away from the table hungry. And, you can hardly wait to come back for more. I'm not sure where she comes up with her recipes. I suspect that she often begins with a basic recipe from the old red and white checkered Betty Crocker Cookbook but ends up adding a dash of this and a dash of that until the flavor is just right.

Judith Ralph

Copper Pennies Marinated Carrots

2 pounds carrots, peeled and sliced
1 teaspoon salt
10¾-ounce can tomato soup, undiluted
1 large onion, diced
1 green bell pepper, diced
½ cup white vinegar
1 cup sugar
¼ cup cooking oil

Cook the carrots and salt in water in a saucepan until tender; drain and set aside. Do not overcook. Combine the remaining ingredients in a saucepan and bring to a rolling boil. Pour over the carrots. Allow the carrots to marinate for several hours, overnight or longer. Serve hot or cold. Keeps in the refrigerator several weeks.

The late Aunt Blanche Rice recipe
Submitted by Anna Sue Ralph Greer

NAMESAKES:

Martha Sue Ralph Edge, and husband Steve, named their daughter, Allie Marie, after Martha's beloved grandmother, Alzera Allie Estelle Ralph.

Kate Elizabeth Edge is Martha and Steve's youngest daughter. The "Elizabeth" comes from Martha's Aunt, Margaret Elizabeth Ralph Payne.

Judy Russell

Corn Casserole

15¼-ounce can whole kernel corn, drained
14¼-ounce can cream-style corn
8-ounce package corn muffin mix
1 cup sour cream
1 stick butter

Combine the corn, corn muffin mix, sour cream and butter in a large bowl. Pour into a 1½-quart greased casserole dish. Bake at 350 degrees for 45 to 60 minutes or until golden brown.

For a number of years several of us have been getting together. Our relationships range from mother, daughter, aunt, cousin, neighbor, childhood friend, and so on. It actually started out as a get together for two or three women who hadn't seen each other in a while. They met at one person's house, stayed up the whole night getting reacquainted and catching up on past news. From there it has grown to about 8 ladies from all walks of life who take a few minutes out of the year to share laughs, memories, and tears.   We've colored each others hair (in our motel room), stayed up all night getting manicures and enduring bikini waxes. Once, we arrived too early for the buffet at a restaurant but chose to wait and wait and wait for it to open (well, we heard the food was to die for). And we've spent many tears crying over family members who were hurting or missing a loved one who had already gone on.

Many dollars have been saved from hiring expensive therapists. Times we've spent sharing scriptures and devotions have been the best therapy money could buy. The good thing about our time together is that whatever is shared in the group stays in the group.

Kim Mitchell

Cowboy Potatoes

1 pound bacon
5 pounds potatoes, washed, sliced thin with peelings
2 medium sweet onions, peeled and sliced
Salt to taste
Pepper to taste
Paprika to taste
4 cups shredded mild Cheddar cheese

Fry the bacon in a large skillet with a lid; remove and drain on a paper towel. Put ½ of the potatoes in the bottom of a skillet with the bacon grease. Layer the onion slices on top of the potatoes. Add the remaining potatoes. Add the salt, pepper, and paprika and cover. Turn often being careful not to burn on one side. Turn the heat to low when the potatoes are thoroughly cooked. Crumble the bacon on top and sprinkle with the cheese on top. Cover until the cheese is melted. Serve 'em up!!!

I have made this recipe twice at my workplace, once for a family whose mother was in the hospital and once for a potluck. They were a rave and I could hardly believe it because the dish was just a simple old camping recipe picked up from Kitty Gray.

Debra Tron

TRAIL-GATING

Debbie Tron and Kitty Gray are two of my trail-riding companions. Just last year at the age of 46 I began the adventure of horseback riding. My husband and I, along with two other couples have ridden rustic trails up and down the rocky hills of Mammoth Cave National Park, through the edge waters of Kentucky Lake and back home across the scenic hills and valleys of Ohio County. We have a small horse trailer with sleeping quarters and have a great time camping out.

We women do most of the cooking, sometimes over a campfire, sometimes in a crock pot, or maybe with an electric skillet. These days campgrounds have electrical hookups. Debbie makes great salmon patties with Mixed Bean Soup and Kitty has become an expert at flipping those blueberry pancakes. The guys really enjoy the breakfasts that we whip up. We have sausage, bacon, eggs, pancakes, gravy and even fried canned biscuits. You just put enough cooking oil in the bottom of an electric skillet to cover, place your biscuits side by side and cover with a lid. Cook on oven temperature until done. Tastes great!!!

Judith Ralph

Campfire Potatoes...Let campfire burn down. Plaster large baking potatoes with mud, about 1/2-inch thick. Place potatoes in red-hot coals for about 30 minutes until mud is rock hard. Crack and remove mud from outside of potatoes. Wash. Split and serve with butter, sour cream, cheese, bacon bits, etc. for a quick fix meal.

Elsie's Dressed Eggs

6 hard-boiled eggs, peeled
¼ cup mayonnaise
1 teaspoon white vinegar
1 teaspoon prepared mustard
½ teaspoon Morton's Nature Seasoning

Cut each egg in half lengthwise. Scoop the yolks out into a bowl.
Add the remaining ingredients and mash using a fork. Put a
spoonful of the mixture back into the egg whites. Chill.

*This recipe for dressed eggs is quite different from my grandparents' but just as
delicious. Every time my sister and I ate with my father and step mom we would
race to see who would be the one to get the last egg. We really enjoyed them.*

Shelia Oliver Thurman

Family Art, the Minnow Trap

In our family, from time to time women have taken on roles traditionally assumed by men. When our family moved back home to Kentucky, our son was 12 years old. He had a real interest in fishing. My dad, Ralph Hobbs, was good at this sport. He even showed me a few tricks of his own, but did not live to share these skills with his grandchildren. Nothing would have pleased him more. So, I passed on from Dad to his grandson, Kinsey Ralph Richards, the family art of making a minnow trap. I instructed Kinsey to take a 3x3-foot square of window screen wire and bring all the corners together. Then sew the edge seams leaving a hole the size of a quarter at the 4 corners. Tuck the ends inside the trap. Tie off at the top with a long thin wire. Place crackers inside. The minnows go inside to feed but they cannot find their way out.

Debra Hobbs Richards

Mother's 1st Stone

I remember the day (probably 30 years ago!) that my mother went outside to find a smooth stone. She wrote the following on it, in black permanent marker: 1st. Then she placed it on the kitchen window sill, where we would be sure to see it everyday. In the Bible, Jesus once said that a person without any sin could throw the "first stone" at a sinner. My mother used that rock to remind us not to judge others without first examining our own hearts. It is still in her kitchen today.

Lisa Young

Grandmother Oliver's Dressed Eggs

6 hard-boiled eggs, peeled
1 tablespoon butter
1 tablespoon sugar
1 tablespoon white vinegar

Cut each egg in half lengthwise. Scoop the yolks out in a bowl.
Add the remaining ingredients and mash using a fork. Put a
spoonful of the mixture back into the egg whites.

*Going to Grandmother and Old Daddy Oliver's house on the farm was always an
exciting time for me. Grandmother was a wonderful cook. We had big Sunday dinners and dressed eggs were always on the table. Serves 12.*

Shelia Thurman

Mama Leach's Fried Green Tomatoes

Green tomatoes, washed and thinly sliced
Cooking oil
Flour
Sugar

Soak the green tomato slices in salt water for 30 minutes and drain. Heat the cooking oil in a large skillet. Dredge the tomato slices in the flour. Place the slices in a hot skillet, one layer at a time. Sprinkle ⅛ teaspoon sugar on top of each tomato slice. Fry slowly until each tomato slice is browned, being careful not to burn. Turn the tomato slices over with sugar side down. Cook slowly until brown and glazed. Drain on paper towel.

Once you have tried these, you will never like fried green tomatoes cooked any other way. The sugar is the secret ingredient!

Anna Mary Leach

Blue Polka Dot Dress

As one grows old, childhood memories seem vague and distant. The mind collects bits and pieces of information that don't always fit together. For example, one of my first memories is of someone in a blue polka dot dress. I remembered the dress well, but that is about all. My oldest sister, Myrtle, later told me that she was the one in the blue polka dot dress and that she was holding me up to watch the train go by.

James Lexter Leach

Mamaw's Noodles

1 large egg
½ egg shell water, about 1 tablespoon
½ cup all-purpose flour
½ cup self-rising flour

Combine all of the ingredients in a bowl and mix well. Dough will be stiff. Roll the dough on a floured surface. Roll the dough very thin and cut into ½-inch strips. Noodles can be cooked immediately or can be dried and frozen for use at a later date.

Mamaw Alvey would always make noodles for our family Christmas. She would begin right after Thanksgiving. She used at least a dozen eggs because there would be 35 to 40 people for dinner. Mamaw Alvey was the world's best noodle maker and everyone loved noodles, even those that married into the family. Mamaw had a special pan she used only for noodles. To this day, anytime my mom cooks noodles, she uses Mamaw's "noodle pan."

Carla Eden

According to the experts, a family tradition gives the child a sense of security.

Mom's Thanksgiving Day Corn Bread Dressing

One 9-inch skillet baked cornbread
2 slices bread, dried
2 to 4 cups turkey or chicken broth
1 onion, finely chopped
2 stalks celery, finely chopped
1 teaspoon sage
1 teaspoon salt
1 teaspoon pepper

Crumble the cornbread and bread slices in a large mixing bowl.
Add 1 cup of the broth, onion, celery and spices and mix well.
Add the remaining broth, a little at a time, to a juicy consistency.
Pour into a 9x13-inch baking dish. Bake at 350 degrees for about
1 hour. Serves 10 to 12.

You may add extra of all of the ingredients according to your family's taste. Our family likes this dressing juicy, however if it is dry you may pour turkey gravy over the top.

Debbie Greene Moxley

Peanut Butter and Banana Sandwiches

Sauce

1 cup sugar
½ cup white vinegar, less 1 tablespoon
1 tablespoon water
2 eggs, beaten
Dash of salt
¼ stick butter

Sandwiches

5 small or 4 large bananas
Creamy or crunchy peanut butter

Combine all of the ingredients for the sauce in a heavy saucepan.
Cook over a low heat until the mixture thickens; stirring constantly
until creamy. Cool.

Cut the bananas into 4 sections. Slice each section lengthwise.
Spread the peanut butter between the slices to make sandwiches.
Place the sandwiches in a glass bowl.   Pour the cooled sauce over
the bananas and serve. Serves 8 to 10.

*This recipe came from my mother-in-law, Christine Boswell. We have always made
it for the holidays. It's a favorite of my girls.*

Shirley Boswell

Potato Casserole

1 stick butter
2-pound bag frozen hash browns, thawed
½ cup chopped onion
10.5-ounce can cream of chicken soup
1 cup sour cream
2 teaspoons salt
1 teaspoon pepper
½ pound shredded sharp Cheddar cheese
Corn flakes, optional

Combine all of the ingredients except the corn flakes in a bowl.
Pour into 9x13-inch buttered casserole dish. Crush the cornflakes
and sprinkle over the top. Bake at 350 degrees for 1 hour.

*A memory of Christmas with the Alveys is when Mamaw used her "wheat" dishes.
The guys would sit at the big table and would all get to use these special dishes.
After Mamaw and Papaw passed away, I got part of the set. Christmas 2005,
I took my "wheat" dishes to my parents' house and we used them for our
Christmas Brunch.*

Carla Eden

Ruby's Sugar Glazed Sweet Potatoes

6 large sweet potatoes, peeled and sliced
2 sticks butter
Sugar to cover, 1 inch thick

Boil the sweet potatoes in a large pan until tender. Spread the
slices on a 12x16-inch baking sheet. Dot the slices with butter.
Cover with the sugar. Bake, uncovered, at 350 degrees for approximately 10 minutes or until the syrup thickens. Serves 12.

*This is a recipe from my mother-in-law, Ruby Ralph. I envision her standing by the
stove with the oven door open, reaching in, and then pulling out that delicious pan of
hot bubbly sweet potatoes. She was always generous when it came to seasoning
her foods.*

Judith Ralph

WHAT'S THE DIFFERENCE?

*I learned how to cook from my mama. I always thought that when you bake
you just stir it...you don't just bake, you fold, you whip...I thought "what's the
difference?" Mama showed me how to knead bread. When I peeled potatoes, I
just took off little pieces at a time. Mama showed me how to hold the knife
and how to take off the peeling in one long piece. She said when you peel an
apple you peel it from both ends.*

*Mama made me cook cornbread 7 times before I got it right. I either burned it
or didn't get it done enough and that's no joke. I was old too, about 16 or 17
years old.*

Connie Ralph Boling

Sarah Hall Branham's Homemade Hot Rolls

Two ¼-ounce envelopes active dry yeast
⅔ cup granulated sugar, divided
¼ cup warm water
1 cup shortening
1½ teaspoons salt
2 cups boiling water
2 eggs, beaten
6 cups self-rising flour, sifted

Dissolve the yeast and 1 tablespoon of the sugar in the water in a small bowl. Combine the shortening, remaining sugar and salt in a mixing bowl. Add the boiling water and stir until the sugar is dissolved and the shortening is melted. Cool 'til lukewarm. Add the yeast mixture. Stir in the eggs and 3 cups of the flour. I don't remember exactly how much flour Granny actually used, but the above ingredients call for 6 cups and only show using 3 cups. Judge as you add the flour, the dough should be stiff, but not dry.

Place a 7-inch round portion of dough into a clean dry, plastic bread bag. Squeeze the excess air out of the bag and tie at the end. Leave enough room, at least ½ of the bag, for the dough to expand. Place the bag in the bottom of the refrigerator overnight or up to 2 nights. You may have at least 2 bags.

Cut open the bag and dust the dough with flour. Pinch off enough dough for 1 roll. Roll it around in your hands to make a ball. Press this down onto a greased cookie sheet using your knuckles. Brush melted margarine over the top of the rolls and let them rise until doubled in size. Bake at 400 degrees for 10 minutes or until browned.

These hot rolls were a staple food at all family functions. Everyone lined up around the oven waiting for the first pan to bake. I would help by brushing the melted butter on the tops. They were best hot out of the oven. The ingredients were estimated, as Granny never measured anything! Her 1_ teaspoons of salt were a sprinkle in the palm of her hand. No one in the family has ever exactly duplicated the taste of these rolls! My Granny died in October 1999 and everyone still remembers the smell and taste of these wonderful hot rolls.

Angela Young

Gaynor Family
From left to right front row: Matthew, Joan,
David, Back row: Bob, Laura, Vickie, Becky

Scalloped Potatoes

⅓ cup chopped onion
5 tablespoons butter
5 tablespoons all-purpose flour
1¼ teaspoons salt
½ teaspoon pepper
5 cups milk
6 cups potatoes, thinly sliced and peeled

Sauté the onion in the butter in a large saucepan until tender. Add the flour, salt and pepper and stir until blended. Add the milk gradually. Bring to a boil; reduce the heat, cook and stir for 2 minutes or until the sauce is thickened.

Place ½ of the potatoes in a greased 3-quart baking dish. Pour ½ of the sauce over the potatoes and repeat. Bake, uncovered, at 350 degrees for 60 to 70 minutes or until the potatoes are tender and the top is slightly browned. Serve immediately. Serves 8.

This is an old recipe learned years ago in a Home Economics class.

Myrl Ralph

Skillet Cabbage

3 tablespoons bacon grease
1 medium red onion, chopped
3 stalks celery, chopped
1 medium head cabbage, chopped
1 green pepper, chopped
2 large tomatoes, chopped
1 teaspoon salt
½ teaspoon black pepper
1 tablespoon sugar
1 pound ground beef or sausage

Heat the bacon grease in a large skillet with a lid. Toss in the vegetables and seasonings and mix well. Cover and cook over a moderate heat until the cabbage is tender. Brown the ground beef in a separate skillet and drain. Add to the vegetables. Simmer for a few minutes to add flavor. I use my electric skillet but any large pot with a cover works just as well.

It's good to remember our ancestors and their way of doing things and their way of life. But it is also important to make new memories for our children and grandchildren and strive to make them good ones.

Kathryn Bailey

Spanish Corn Bread

3 eggs, well beaten
⅔ cup cooking oil
2 cups self-rising corn meal
1 tablespoon baking soda
1 tablespoon salt
3 tablespoons all-purpose flour
1 cup milk
1 cup chopped onions
1 cup chopped green pepper
15-ounce can cream-style corn
1 cup shredded American cheese

Combine all of the ingredients except the cheese in a large bowl. Pour ½ of the batter into a greased 10-inch cast-iron skillet. Spread the cheese over the batter. Pour the remaining batter over the cheese. Bake at 400 degrees for 45 minutes.

For Hot Mexican Cornbread substitute jalapeño pepper for the green pepper.

My first memory of cooking was in the early 1950s. My mother, Velma Leach Miller, taught me to make corn bread. Mama worked at the GE factory in Owensboro and my older sister, Emogene, and I had to help prepare the suppertime meal. My job was to make the corn bread. I also made this for the Sunday meal, but of course, it was plain corn bread.

Jerl Dean Adkins

Treasured Cabbage Rolls

3 heads cabbage
2 pounds ground beef
1 pound sausage
1 onion, chopped
3 eggs
6-ounce can tomato paste
Two 16-ounce cans sauerkraut
Two 16-ounce cans diced tomatoes

Boil the cabbage in a large pot until the leaves are tender and fall off the head. Set aside to cool. Combine the ground beef, sausage, onion, eggs and tomato paste in a bowl. Form the mixture into several large egg shapes. Wrap the shapes in the cabbage leaves, using toothpicks to secure the cabbage. Place the shaped cabbage into the bottom of a Dutch oven. Layer the sauerkraut and diced tomatoes over the shaped cabbage. Repeat. Bake at 350 degrees for 1½ to 2 hours. This must be served with great homemade mashed potatoes.

New Year's Day is one of our family's favorite holidays. Throughout my life we've celebrated New Year's with a tradition I thought started generations ago. I was surprised when researching that my mom, Joan Huddy, actually began this tradition. Each New Year's Day she would fix cabbage rolls and hide dimes inside each of them. She would bake them in her Club Aluminum Dutch oven. The year that was being celebrated determined the number of dimes hidden. If you were fortunate enough to fine the charred dime, you were assured to have a year of prosperity. Even though mom passed away several years ago, (Dad, Vickie, Laura, David, Matt, their families and mine,) we resolved to carry on the tradition she created. We still use the same Club Aluminum Dutch oven to bake our cabbage rolls. Our menu always consists of the cabbage rolls and mashed potatoes. It is the one day out of the year that our children are willing to eat cooked cabbage, all in the spirit of finding the "treasured" dime. As soon as the last dime is found, everyone mysteriously becomes "full."

Becky Gaynor

Turkey Gravy

2 to 3 tablespoons vegetable oil
1 to 2 tablespoons self-rising flour
2 to 4 cups turkey or chicken broth

Heat the oil in a skillet over a medium heat. Add the flour and brown. Add the broth and stir quickly until it bubbles. Turn off the heat until ready to serve. Add more broth or water if the gravy is too thick.

My mom, Sue Greene, was famous for her Thanksgiving meal. Everything was always made from scratch. All of the kids made their favorite dish. The table was set with linens and Dad carved the turkey. Now for Thanksgiving with my family I set the table with linens and make sure everybody's favorite dish is on the table. Thanks Mom for our tradition.

Debbie Greene Moxley

THINGS MOTHERS SAY...
(As shared by Bro. David Britt on Mother's Day 2006)

Be careful you will put your eye out!
If someone told you to jump off a cliff would you do it?
You have enough dirt behind your ears to grow potatoes.
Close that door, were you raised in a barn?
Don't put that in your mouth you don't know where it has been!

September 1964
Grandma (Velma Miller) with Barry Lynn and
Judith Moseley, Debra and Russ Hobbs

In Loving Memory of
Velma Leach Miller

September 22, 1916 – July 5, 1974

The good Lord really smiled upon me when he chose to place me in a family with one of the world's most precious humans, my grandma, Velma Leach Miller. She was grandma to a total of six. I was the oldest, her first born grandchild and was allowed to spend a good deal of my childhood in her presence. She loved her family more than life itself. She knew God had blessed her and shared her blessings with our church and community.

In order to help feed her family she raised large gardens and put up grape juice, apples and pears. The woman had patience. She never objected when I ate as many apples as I could hold while she was preparing them to can. That's real love!

Christmas at Grandma's was the most spectacular event of the whole year. Grandma would work so hard. Her house glowed with shining tinsel, bright lights, and especially the angel on top of the real cedar tree. She thought of it all from candied orange slices, coconut bonbons, chocolate cream drops and peanut brittle, mixed nuts in the shell and fresh fruit, down to the coconut we all shared at the end of the night. Hand wrapped gifts tied off with curly Q ribbons were decorated with care. Just as much thought went into the contents inside the boxes of goodies as the wrapping on the outside. Usually a guest from the North Pole would some-how find his way to my grandma's house. He, too, knew just how special Grandma's house was!

Preparations for Christmas supper started days earlier. A time or two I was lucky enough to go on the trip to the big town of "Owensboro" for most of our groceries were purchased at the White Front store in our little town, Fordsville. But, the turkey, the oysters for stuffing and the fresh cranberries were another story. Grandma went to Owensboro on a quest to find the biggest bird in the store freezer. We would always pick through 'til we found the perfect turkey suited for our royal family. Our trip was well worth the trouble when the juicy bird was pulled from the oven and its delicious aroma filtered throughout the big old house at Grandma's.

Debra Hobbs Richards

BEVERAGES

Barbara Garland, Elza Motley, Phyllis Jean Blanton, and Bill Motley

My cousins and I spent many summers with our Grandma Motley. One of the biggest treats was the fun of going across the street to Lawrence Jones' Grocery. She would let us get anything we wanted and then put it on her "tab."

Kim Mitchell

To My Mother

There is a sweet song
ringing throughout the heavens,
a song sung by angels,
a song about mothers.

A mother is the strength
of the mighty oak
standing firm
against restless winds.

A mother is the hope
of a welcomed rainbow
smiling brightly
amongst storm tossed skies.

A mother is the nourishment
of a cool spring rain
steadily falling
upon a barren earth.

A mother is the persistence
of a gentle breeze
softly caressing
fields of green.

A mother is the love
God gave to his children,
a love that never dies,
a love that grows through others.

Judith Moseley Ralph

Banana Slush

4 cups sugar
6 cups water
46-ounce can pineapple juice
12-ounce can frozen orange juice, thawed
12-ounce can frozen lemonade, thawed
5 bananas, mashed
6 quarts ginger ale

Dissolve the sugar completely in the water in a large bowl. Add the juices and bananas and mix well. Pour the mixture in 3 half-gallon containers with crumpled waxed paper on the top and freeze. The waxed paper helps keep the bananas under the liquid so they will not turn dark. When ready to thaw place the frozen mixture in a punch bowl and pour the ginger ale over the top. Mix to a slushy consistency. Serves 50.

When my daughter, Jamie, married Barry Johnston, I made this slush for the wedding reception because it was easy to freeze ahead of time. I made this mixture a month in advance and froze it. Then 24 hours before the reception I put it in the refrigerator.

Joyce Leach

Jamie Leach,
Tamara and
Teresa Miller

Christmas Ice Ring

Fill a 6-cup ring mold ⅔ full with water. Alternate orange wedges, peeling side down with red and green maraschino cherries, using 3 at a time in a group. Add a layer of water carefully. Freeze for 30 minutes or until oranges and cherries are firmly in place. Slowly add water to the top to freeze. Run hot water on the sides of the mold when ready to remove and the ring should slide out easily. Great for holiday punch recipes.

Heather Litsey

On December 7, 1946, my sister, Emogene, her girl friend and I were playing when Papa Leach came to our house and insisted we go with him to his house. Later that day Papa took us back home. To our surprise when we entered the house my sister and I saw Grandmother Miller holding a newborn baby boy close to the hot, pot-belly stove. I thought she was going to burn him up. While we were away visiting, the stork had brought us a baby brother. We had no idea that Mama was expecting. I was 7 years old and Emogene was 8 years old!

Emogene, Wayne and Jerl Dean Miller

Jerl Dean Miller Adkins

Grandma Harrel's Spice Tea

14-ounce package orange-flavored instant drink mix
2 cups sugar
2 teaspoons cloves, optional
⅔ cup instant tea granules
2 teaspoons cinnamon
3-ounce package lemonade drink mix

Combine all of the ingredients and store in airtight container.
Add 3 teaspoons of the mixture to one cup of hot water for a cup
of tea.

From Grandma Harrel, Christmas 2003
Heather Litsey

Mamaw Laura

I lived next door to Mamaw and Granddad Hall for as long as I can remember as a child. My brother and I spent many nights at their house. Mamaw and I would always get up earlier than everyone to have Taster's Choice Instant coffee, and sugar cookies, those big ones with the sprinkles on top. Mamaw Laura told me so many stories about her childhood and about her life with Granddad Homer. Although I can't remember every story she told, I will always be grateful for the time she took to share those memories with me.

Kellie Hall Ralph

Southern Sweet Tea

5 cups water
6 regular-size tea bags
1¼ cups sugar

Bring the water to a boil in a saucepan. Add the tea bags and
remove the pan from the heat. Allow the tea to steep for 15 or
more minutes. Add the sugar to a 2-quart glass pitcher. Pour the
tea over the sugar and stir until the sugar is dissolved. Fill the
pitcher to the top with water and stir again. Serve the tea over ice.

Kim Mitchell

Elza Motley

When I think of the women who have made a
difference in my life, the first one who comes to
mind is my mom. She showed me, as well as
taught me, how to love my family. She loved
unconditionally. She sacrificed everything for us.
She never had anything bad to say of anyone.
At her funeral many came by to say, "Elza Motley
never had a bad word to say of anyone."

Judy Back

Tropical Ice

8½-ounce can crushed pineapple, including juice
2 cups mashed bananas
2 cups orange juice
2 tablespoons lemon juice
12 maraschino cherries
1 cup sugar
Dash of salt

Combine all of the ingredients in a medium bowl. Pour the mixture into 2 refrigerator ice cube trays. Freeze until almost solid. Remove the cubes into a bowl and beat using an electric mixer to make fluffy. Freeze for several hours. Spoon into 12-ounce glass and fill with your favorite beverage.

Ginger Jiffy:

Spoon 2 or 3 big chunks of Tropical Ice into a glass. Add chilled ginger ale and stir.

Cola Jiffy:

Spoon 2 or 3 big chunks of Tropical Ice into a glass. Add chilled cola and stir.

Dairy Punch:

Spoon 2 or 3 big chunks of Tropical Ice into a glass. Add chilled milk and stir.

Fruit Cooler:

Mix tropical ice and cold water, _ of each.

Thelma Matthews

Flora Miller,
Ida Bellamy,
Amanda Lindsey
and Jossie Whitler

In Loving Memory of
Flora Keown Miller
July 12, 1879 to
March 3, 1964

To My Loving Grandmother Miller,

To me you were always a kind, little, stooped, old woman with spectacles, arthritis and bunions. A widow in an old house with no indoor plumbing. A well to draw water from and an old whiskey barrel to catch rain water. There were always 'wiggle tails' in that barrel.

You were satisfied with an ice box, wood cook stove with a water tank on the side for hot water, iron bedsteads with feather beds and a wicker rocker.

I remember the Sunday meals you cooked. There were homemade biscuits, a large pitcher of lime Kool-aid and a fresh pie from the pie safe.

My sister and I loved to spend the night with you. We got to go to the store and pick what we wanted to eat. Our favorite was Vienna sausages. It was also a treat to get a soft drink. You bought Dr. Pepper because the company had a promotion that if they came to your house and you had a Dr. Pepper they would give you a silver dollar. They came one day and you got the silver dollar.

You were usually quilting on a quilt frame set up in your front room. I tried to use a needle and thimble to help you. Your quilts were special gifts to us grandkids at 8th and 12th grade graduations and at weddings.

In the hot summertime we watched for you coming down the sidewalk from town carrying dripping ice cream cones for us.

You wanted no luxuries for yourself, but you saved to buy saving bonds for us.

Later, with failing eyesight you could be found in the front porch swing hoping for a visit from your great-grandkids. After drinking cases of carrot juice you still went blind but loved to touch and rub the heads of your great-grandkids.

Only good memories remain of a grandmother who loved and spoiled her grandkids.

Your Loving Granddaughter,
Jerl Dean Miller Adkins

BREAKFAST

Grandma and the Grandkids:
Michael in back, Anthony, Grandma Judy, Madison, Daniel, and Blair.

Mom has always enjoyed her grandchildren. With each one she made cooking fun: World Famous Pancakes with Madison and Blair, Heath Bar Pie with Daniel, Peanut Butter Fudge with Anthony and a stocked refrigerator of soft drinks for Michael. We have since added Ella to our family. She looks forward to making her favorites as well.

Kim Mitchell

Sausages, you know those round kind...

Austin came into our life as a small toddler, 16 months of age. He quickly became the child of my heart. Today he is 4 years old and loves to come to Mamaw's house to spend the night and help cook his favorite evening meal, "sausages, you know those round kind, scrambled eggs, and gravy, can I stir it?" Austin stands on a step stool beside the stove while I am close at hand. He cracks then slides the eggs into a bowl, stirs them with a fork, and pours the eggs into a buttered skillet. I scramble the eggs. Austin asks a lot of questions. When the eggs are done he dips them onto his plate. Next, he then pours milk into the gravy skillet and stirs until it is hot and begins to thicken. That's when I take over. While the gravy cools, I place a couple of link sausages in the microwave. Austin closes the door and turns on the microwave. When the meal is complete, we enjoy...

Soon Austin is going to have a little brother or sister (the doctor says a girl). There will always be room in the kitchen for one more!!!

Mamaw
(Judith Ralph)

With great anticipation I await the birth of a new generation. Our first biological grandchild, Allie, is due to be born to Andy and Heather in September of this year. Julie and Jimmy are expecting the birth of our second in February of 2007.

Judith Ralph

Anna's Chocolate Gravy

1 tablespoon cocoa
3 tablespoons self-rising flour
3 tablespoons sugar
Dash of salt
1 cup milk
Chunk of margarine, approximately 1 tablespoon

Combine the dry ingredients in a saucepan, add the milk and stir. Add the margarine and stir until the margarine is melted. Cook over a medium heat.

When I was in the first grade and beyond, I would get car sick riding to school. My mother, Anna Leach, wanted me to have something in my stomach, to be able to think and study in school. She discovered I could eat and keep down chocolate gravy over white bread. For years, she patiently made this for me each morning. It was like having chocolate pie for breakfast everyday! But it worked!!!

Brenda Young

Blair's Monkey Bread

7½-ounce can refrigerated biscuits
2 teaspoons cinnamon
3 teaspoons sugar
1 stick butter or margarine, melted

Preheat the oven to 325 degrees. Separate the biscuits. Roll each biscuit into a ball. Combine the cinnamon and sugar in a small bowl. Roll the balls in the cinnamon mixture. Place the balls in a 9-inch round greased cake pan. Pour the butter over the biscuits. Bake for 20 minutes.

Mommy made this recipe for her preschoolers. Then she taught my sister Madison and me how to make it. It's really good.

Blair Back
6 years old

Reg's Cornmeal Gravy

8 slices bacon
1 cup cornmeal
½ teaspoon salt
½ teaspoon pepper
1 cup milk

Fry the bacon over a medium heat in a skillet. Remove the bacon and add the cornmeal, salt and pepper stirring constantly. Add the milk and bring to a boil, continuing to stir until thickened. Serve over hot biscuits or corn bread.

Redgey Back

Chocolate Breakfast Gravy

1½ cups sugar
2 heaping forks or 1/4 cup flour
3 heaping forks or 1/4 cup cocoa
1½ cups milk

Combine the dry ingredients in a bowl. Warm the milk over a low heat in a medium saucepan, being careful not to scorch. Add the dry ingredients and bring to a boil. Boil over a low heat until thickened. Serve over hot buttered biscuits.

As a child I can remember running down the dirt path to Mamaw and Granddad Hall's house. I carried an empty bowl so Mamaw Laura could mix the dry ingredients together as if it were a secret recipe. Then I would hurry home with the mixture so Mom could finish making the chocolate gravy for our breakfast.

Kellie Hall Ralph

To Emogene Moseley 1993

Mamaw you have took care of me for a lot of day and you are nice and always cooked food for us on Sunday its always good to. I have a good life from yur duather and a good uncle from your son you are a nice person I have always liked you and I always will.

Love Robert Ralph

Roses are Red
Violets are Blue
Sugar is Sweat
So are You,

I Love You MAMAW

Egg's Nest

1 slice bread
1 tablespoon butter, softened
1 egg, whole

Cut a hole in the center of the bread slice. Butter both sides of the bread generously. Place the bread in a hot skillet. Crack the egg into the hole. Cook until desired doneness. Flip and brown.

Mom used to make Egg's Nest for me at breakfast before school. I was always a sleepy head and would take awhile to rouse out of bed, but Mom with her unlimited patience would come to the door 2 or 3 times and tell me to get up. When I finally went to the kitchen, my breakfast plate was always waiting for me at the bar.

Judith Ralph

Burn Out

Mama tried to burn me out on eggs one time and I ate 27 eggs. Once for dinner I ate 7 chocolate pies. Mama could cook!!!

James O. Ralph, Sr

Mrs. Minnie's Sausage Rolls
Great for Breakfast, Brunch, or Appetizer

2¾ cups biscuit mix
⅔ cup milk
1 pound sausage, at room temperature

Preheat the oven to 400 degrees. Combine 2¼ cups of the biscuit mix and the milk using a fork until a soft dough forms. Sprinkle the remaining biscuit mix on a clean, dry surface. Roll out the dough, coating with the biscuit mix. Roll the dough into a very thin rectangle shape using a rolling pin. Spread the sausage evenly over the dough making sure to reach the edges. Gently roll the dough into a long log, beginning with the longest end, approximately 18 to 20 inches long, shaping as you go. Cut the roll in half for easier handling. Wrap the rolls in waxed paper or aluminum foil. Refrigerate for 30 to 60 minutes for easy slicing. Slice and place on a baking sheet. Bake at 400 degrees for 10 to 12 minutes or until brown on top. You can store this in the refrigerator for up to 2 weeks.

My mother, who was a wonderful cook, handed this recipe down to me. She would make this on special occasions and it was always a big hit with our family.

Maggie Ring

There was a story, which I've treasured, shared about Mrs. Minnie Hall by one of her daughters, Mary. Minnie was a godly woman and faithful to her church. Apparently when Minnie was at home in the evening with her girls, she would begin reading her Bible. It never failed that during her reading she would just be "stumped" as to where to find a scripture in the Bible and would call on all the girls to begin helping her look for it. It took the girls a while to catch on that Minnie was cleverly luring her daughters into her personal Bible study.

Kim Mitchell

Poached Egg

Butter
Egg

Butter the cup in the top portion of egg poacher. Fill the bottom portion of the egg poacher about 1_ inches deep with water. Crack the egg, careful not to break the yolk and drop the egg in the cup. Simmer for 3 to 5 minutes or to desired doneness.

When I was a little boy I always thought that I had a city grandma living in the city and a country grandma living in the country. I was amused by the fact that Mamaw Miller lived inside the city limits of Fordsville within walking distance of Jack Edge Grocery and Feed Store, the Whitefront Grocery and Junie Royal's Hardware Store. The Tasty Freeze was just around the bend. Sometimes Mamaw would drive me to the Tasty Freeze and give me a quarter to buy a milkshake.   For breakfast I had poached eggs, biscuits out of a can or toasted pop tarts.

Mamaw Moseley lived on the outskirts of Whitesville and did not drive. At my country grandma's house I always had fresh eggs, homemade biscuits, and country ham or homemade sausage for breakfast. When I visited her house she would let me go to the hen house to get my own egg to scramble. I was fascinated by the chickens. Papaw Moseley didn't like the idea because he was afraid I would disturb the hens but I went anyway.

Barry Moseley

World Famous Pancakes

2 eggs
2 cups self-rising flour
¼ cup sugar
1 cup milk
⅓ cup vegetable oil

Beat the eggs in a large bowl. Combine the flour and sugar; add to the eggs. Add the milk and vegetable oil, beating until the mixture is smooth. Pour about ¼ cup batter for each pancake, onto a hot, lightly greased griddle. Turn the pancakes when the tops are covered with bubbles and the edges look cooked. Serve with your favorite syrup.

Once I was big enough to be at the kitchen counter with Grandma Judy, she let me make pancakes. When I would spend the night with her we always knew what we were going to have for breakfast, pancakes. She and I finally named them "World Famous Pancakes."

Madison Back
Age 10

CAKES

The Mitchell family at the annual Square Club Picnic in Fern Creek, KY. Each year Buren and Ruby Bandy hosted this event where you were sure to sample a variety of homemade desserts.

Kim Mitchell

Kentucky Girl

My daughter, Sara, and I share a love of cooking and good food. When she was small she always wanted to help me prepare dinner. One of the sweetest memories I have is of her standing on a stool right beside me at the stove, stirring a pot. After high school she decided to go to culinary school and become a chef, a pastry chef.

She is currently working in England and though I miss her terribly, I am so proud of her. At 24 years of age I would never have had the courage to leave behind all that I knew and go to work 6000 miles from home. This has been an experience she will someday share with her children and grandchildren and maybe her courage will inspire the next generation to take a chance and take that leap of faith.

When her job ends in July, I look forward to having her home for a visit, so we can stand side-by-side at the stove once more and talk about all of her future dreams. Dreams that I'm certain she will make a reality.

Becky Reaves

Sara is the Assistant Pastry Chef at the Montagu Arms Hotel in Beaulieu, New Forest, Hampshire, England.

Apple Spice Custard Cake

18¼-ounce box spice cake mix
2 medium Gala apples, peeled and finely chopped
14-ounce can sweetened condensed milk
8 ounces sour cream, room temperature
¼ cup lemon juice
Cinnamon to taste
Prepared whipped topping, optional

Preheat the oven to 350 degrees. Prepare the cake mix according to the package directions. Stir in the apples. Pour into a well greased and floured 9x13-inch baking dish. Bake for 30 to 40 minutes until a toothpick comes out clean. Do not over cook. Combine the sweetened condensed milk, sour cream and lemon juice in a medium bowl. Spread the mixture over the top of the warm cake. Return to the oven and bake for 10 minutes or until set. Remove from the oven and sprinkle with the cinnamon. Top with the whipped topping. Keep refrigerated if you add whipped topping.

Anetta Mollohan

Watering Place

Grandma (Martha) Stinnett, took her family to the resorts or watering places as was fashionable at that time. She never had to cook as she always had a black mammy.

The Late Bill Moseley

Baba's Lemon Cake

Cake

20-ounce box lemon cake mix
3-ounce box lemon instant pudding mix
¾ cup vegetable oil
¾ cup water
4 eggs

Preheat the oven to 350 degrees. Combine all of the ingredients in a bowl. Pour into a   prepared 9x13-inch pan. Bake for 35 to 40 minutes. Remove from the oven and punch lots of holes in the cake using a toothpick or fork.

Glaze

2 cups powdered sugar
½ cup lemon juice
2 tablespoons melted butter
2 tablespoons water

Combine all of the ingredients in a small saucepan and heat. Pour over the hot cake. Let the cake cool and serve. Sprinkle the cake with more powdered sugar, if desired.

My grandmother (Baba) died in 2005, and I am so thankful that I got this recipe from her, in her own handwriting. She didn't bake much as she got older, but she always tried to fix this easy cake for me when I came to visit.

Lisa Young

Baked Alaska

18¼-ounce box chocolate cake mix
¾ cup egg whites, approximately 6 to 8
½ teaspoon cream of tartar
1 cup sugar
1 gallon vanilla ice cream, sliced

Prepare the cake mix according to the package directions in a 9x13-inch pan. Cool and remove to a wooden board. Beat the egg whites and cream of tartar in a bowl until foamy. Beat in the sugar gradually. Beat until soft peaks form. Place the ice cream on top of the cake and cover completely with the meringue. Bake at 500 degrees for 3 to 5 minutes.

This recipe was taken from a cookbook my daughter compiled as a freshman home economics student at Ohio County High School. Julie has always had an interest in cooking and especially enjoys preparing special dishes for the holidays. At age 14, she decided to make Baked Alaska for our Christmas Dinner. I will never forget the big smile on her face when she pulled it from the oven. It was delicious.

Judith Ralph

Jimmy Ralph and sister, Blanche

My great aunt, Blanche Ralph Rice, lived with us for several years until she passed away at 96 years of age. She was a wonderful person and she lived a long good life. She loved books and would read anything and everything she could find. Aunt Blanche was a teacher at a girl's school and taught secretarial skills. When I get up in age I hope to be half the person she was. She is greatly missed by all.

She had this old cookbook that I cherish but the pages are yellowed and crumbly so I handle it with care. The Brown Sugar Crumb Cake (next page) is one of the recipes from that cookbook. Note the date at the end of the recipe.

Debra Taylor

Brown Sugar Crumb Cake

2½ cups cake flour
2½ teaspoons baking powder
½ teaspoon salt
½ cup butter or shortening
¾ cup firmly packed brown sugar
1 cup finely cut raisins
1 egg, well beaten
¾ cup milk
2 tablespoons sugar
⅛ teaspoon cinnamon

Sift the flour once and measure. Add the baking powder and salt. Sift 3 times. Cream the butter thoroughly. Add the sugar gradually and cream until light and fluffy. Work in the flour mixture reserving ¾ cup. Add the raisins to the mixture and mix well. Combine the egg and milk and add gradually to the flour mixture, mixing well. Turn into a greased 8x8-inch pan. Sprinkle with the reserved flour mixture; then with mixture of sugar and cinnamon. Bake at 350 degrees for 50 minutes or until done.

Frances Lee Barton's Class in Home Baking
General Foods Cooking School of the Air
September 20, 1934

From the cookbook of the late Blanche Rice
Submitted by Debra Taylor

Cherry Dump Cake

Two 21-ounce cans cherry pie filling
18½-ounce box yellow cake mix
2 sticks butter, melted

Pour the cherry pie filling into a 9x13-inch baking dish and spread evenly over the bottom. Pour the dry cake mix over the top of the cherries and spread evenly. Drizzle the melted butter over the cake mix using a spoon. Bake at 350 degrees for about 45 minutes, or until the top is golden brown.

Zonia Carman

Little Julie

For special occasions the Ralph family gathers at Papaw Ralph's place for a big feast. The daughters and daughter-in-laws are responsible for preparing most of the food. Zonia makes a great Dump Cake. Connie usually brings Chocolate éclair or fruit salad. Martha's specialty is introducing new recipes. Most often I bring barbecue pork or some other type of meat. However, Andrew always leaves the potato mashing to his grand daughter, my daughter, Julie. It seems that no one else can quite make them to suit Papaw's taste like "Little Julie" can.

Judith Ralph

Chocolate Fudge Cake

2 squares unsweetened chocolate
½ cup shortening
½ cup brown sugar
½ cup granulated sugar
½ cup water
1 egg, beaten
1 cup all-purpose flour
½ teaspoon baking powder
½ teaspoon salt
½ teaspoon baking soda, combined with ¼ cup buttermilk
1 teaspoon vanilla extract

Preheat the oven to 350 degrees. Melt the chocolate and shortening in a saucepan. Add the sugars and water and bring to a boil. Remove from the heat and let cool slightly. Add the egg, beating continuously. Sift the flour, measure and sift again with the baking powder and salt. Add the flour to the chocolate mixture alternately with the remaining ingredients and beat until smooth. Pour into greased and floured 8x8-inch pan. Bake for 25 minutes.

Fudge Sauce

1 square unsweetened chocolate
1 cup cold coffee
1 cup sugar
3 tablespoons cornstarch
¼ teaspoon salt
2 teaspoons vanilla extract
2 tablespoons butter or margarine
⅓ cup heavy cream

Combine the first 5 ingredients in a saucepan. Stir over a low heat until the chocolate is melted or until the mixture is smooth and thickened, approximately 5 minutes. Cool and stir in the vanilla extract, butter and cream. Pour over the cake.

Kathryn Mitchell

ETERNITY

I am 87 years old and have lived a long and good life, but life is short at the very longest. You wake up one morning and realize that most of your life has passed you by. This life is just a dressing place to prepare you for eternity, forever and ever.

Lorene Leach Wright

Fruit Cocktail Cake

Cake

2 cups self-rising flour
2 eggs, beaten
1½ cups sugar
16-ounce can fruit cocktail, drained
1 cup brown sugar
1 cup chopped pecans

Combine the flour, eggs, sugar and fruit cocktail in a bowl. Pour into a greased and floured 9x13-inch baking pan. Sprinkle with the brown sugar and pecans. Bake at 350 degrees for 35 minutes.

Topping

¾ cup sugar
1 stick margarine
½ cup evaporated milk
6 or 7-ounce can flaked coconut
1 teaspoon vanilla extract

Combine the sugar, margarine and evaporated milk in a saucepan. Bring to a boil and boil for 5 minutes. Add the coconut and vanilla extract. Pour this hot mixture over the cake. Serve the cake or save it; it just gets better. Serves 12.

From the cookbook of the late Virginia Saltzman
Myrl Saltzman Ralph

Gelatin Cake

18-ounce box white cake mix
1 cup boiling water
3-ounce package strawberry gelatin
8-ounce container prepared whipped topping

Prepare the cake mix according to the package directions in a
9x13-inch cake pan.   Cool for 10 minutes and poke holes in the
top of cake about 1 inch apart using the end of a wooden spoon.
Pour the boiling water over the strawberry gelatin in a bowl. Stir
until gelatin is dissolved. Pour the gelatin mixture over the cake.
Allow cake to cool completely and frost with the whipped topping.
Keep refrigerated.

*Makes a delicious light dessert. My (step) great-grandmother, Kathryn Miller, was
the first to bring it to our family gatherings.*

Julie Ralph Alford

REFLECTIONS OF ME

*When my daughter, Julie, was born, I would sometimes reach
into the crib to pick her up and would see myself. Now that
Julie is all grown up and chauffeurs me around, I often feel as
though she is me behind the steering wheel and that I am my
mother in the passenger's seat.*

Judith Ralph

Grandma's Banana Cake

18¼-ounce box yellow cake mix
4 eggs
1 cup water
1 stick margarine, melted
3.4-ounce box banana instant pudding
1 teaspoon banana flavoring

Combine the first 4 ingredients. Add the pudding and flavoring and mix for about 1 minute using an electric mixer. Pour into three 9-inch round cake pans and bake at 350 degrees for 35 minutes or until the cake springs back when you touch it. Remove the cake from the pans and cool.

Icing

3 cups sugar
12-ounce can evaporated milk
2 to 3 medium-size bananas, sliced

Combine the sugar and milk in a saucepan. Cook over a medium-high heat to soft-ball stage. This will take about 14 minutes. Remove from the heat and beat until it loses its gloss. Over beating or it will cause it to become brittle and under beating will cause it to not set up. This is the most important thing about this cake. Frost one layer with the icing. Arrange the sliced bananas on top. Repeat with the remaining layers.

My grandmother brought this to every get-together. It was never very pretty, but it was so moist and delicious! Now that she is gone, someone always manages to bring it to family gatherings. It would not be the same without Grandma's Banana Cake.

Pam Allard

Ice Box Cake

1 stick margarine, softened
1 cup self-rising flour
½ cup chopped pecans
2 tablespoons sugar
8-ounce package cream cheese, softened
1 cup powdered sugar
1 cup prepared non-dairy topping
Two 3.9-ounce packages instant chocolate pudding
3 cups milk
Chocolate chips or nuts, optional

Preheat the oven to 350 degrees. Combine the margarine, flour, pecans and sugar. Pat into a 9x13-inch pan and bake for 15 minutes. Brown under the broiler for 1 minute. Combine the cream cheese, powdered sugar and non-dairy topping. Pour over the crust. Combine the pudding and milk, stirring until thickened. Pour over the cream cheese layer. Top with remaining non-dairy topping. Garnish with the chocolate chips or nuts. Refrigerate.

Carla Eden

Who Made the Kraut?

My Granny could make the best kraut ever. We would take a jar out of the refrigerator and eat it all. My Mom would make it and we would tell her "this isn't as good as Granny's." After telling Mom that several times, little did we know, she would take her kraut over to Granny's. We wouldn't know it was Mom's kraut and we would eat it, thinking Granny had made it.

Carla Eden

Mama's
Chocolate Sauce for Cake

4 tablespoons sugar
1 heaping tablespoon cocoa
1½ cups water
2 teaspoons butter
¼ teaspoon vanilla extract

Combine the sugar and cocoa in a saucepan. Add the water gradually. Bring to a boil and boil over a medium heat for 20 to 25 minutes, thickening to a sauce consistency. Remove from the heat. Add the butter and vanilla extract. Serve warm over cake.

Sometimes cake wouldn't go over as well as pie at our house, but it was always eaten when Mama (Anna Leach) made chocolate sauce to pour over a slice of leftover cake.

Shelia Thurman

Another tip for storing and eating leftover cake I learned from Heather Litsey. She places leftover cake in the refrigerator then removes and heats it in the microwave just until the icing melts and the cake is slightly warm. Makes a moist and delicious dessert!!!

Judith Ralph

Mamaw Punch's Carrot Cake

Cake

18-ounce box carrot cake mix

Prepare the cake mix according to the package directions in a 9x13-inch cake pan. Cool and poke holes in the top of the cake using the handle of a wooden spoon.

Icing

1 cup sugar
1 stick butter
12-ounce can evaporated milk
1 teaspoon vanilla extract

Combine all of the ingredients in a medium saucepan. Cook until the icing thickens, stirring constantly. Remove from the heat. Pour the icing over the cake while hot.

Pamela Ralph Howard

Mamaw Punch

Mamaw Punch ate a fried egg, toast and a bowl of oats with Karo syrup poured over them every morning before she went to work at Johnson Packing Company. She didn't like milk. When she came to our house she didn't have Karo syrup so Mama made sugar molasses and added chocolate to it...water, sugar and cocoa mix. For breakfast on the farm, Mamaw ate bacon or sausage and oats with Mama's chocolate syrup poured over the top.

Connie Ralph Boling

Mom's Baked Cheesecake

CRUST

¼ cup butter
¼ cup sugar
1¼ cups graham cracker crumbs

FILLING

Two 8-ounce packages cream cheese
3-ounce package cream cheese
3 eggs
1½ cups sugar
¾ cup milk
½ teaspoon vanilla extract

Preheat the oven to 375 degrees. Combine the butter, sugar and graham cracker crumbs and press into a springform pan. Blend the cream cheese and eggs until smooth and creamy. Add the sugar and beat until smooth. Add the milk and vanilla extract and beat well. Pour into the crust. Bake for 60 minutes.

TOPPING

½ pint sour cream
3 tablespoons sugar
1 teaspoon vanilla extract

Combine all of the ingredients in a bowl and blend well. Pour over the center of the cheesecake while the cake is hot, leaving a 1-inch border around the edge. Put the cheesecake back into the oven and bake for 10 additional minutes. Refrigerate.

Mrs. Jessie Stephens
Submitted by Jacqueline Merkle

Mom's Cheesecake
(Light and Fluffy)

Two 3-ounce boxes lemon-flavored gelatin
2 cups sugar
Two 8-ounce packages cream cheese
Two 13-ounce cans evaporated milk, chilled

CRUST

1½ cups graham cracker crumbs
¼ cup sugar
¼ cup melted butter or margarine

Dissolve the gelatin in 1⅓ cups hot water. Let cool but do not refrigerate. Combine the sugar and cream cheese in a bowl. Whip the evaporated milk, in a separate bowl, until very thick. Combine the gelatin and cream cheese mixture and mix well. Pour into the milk and mix well. Combine the graham cracker crumbs, sugar and melted butter and place in the bottom of a 9x13-inch pan. Pour the cake mixture into the graham cracker crust. Chill until set.

This makes such a large container of cake that unless I am having a very large group I cut the recipe in half. It fits nicely in an 8x8-inch glass dish. I usually put the can of milk in the freezer for a few minutes to get it colder. It will whip quicker.

Mrs. Jessie once was asked what was the most important lesson she had learned in life. Her answer was to "always remember to put God first, live for Him, respect Him, and do what He would have you to do."

Jacqueline Merkle

WOW: My most difficult lesson to learn was that if you want to be loved you must show love because love is to be shared.

Mrs. Jessie Stephens, age 90.

Pecan Pumpkin Torte
Golden Whisk Award

CAKE

2 cups crushed vanilla wafers
1 cup chopped pecans
½ cup butter, divided
18-ounce package carrot cake mix
1 cup canned pumpkin
¼ cup butter
3 eggs
2 tablespoons water

FILLING

3 cups powdered sugar
⅔ cup butter
4 ounces cream cheese
2 teaspoons vanilla extract
¼ cup caramel ice cream topping
1 cup pecan halves

Preheat the oven to 350 degrees. Combine the wafer crumbs, pecans and ⅓ cup butter in a large bowl. Beat at a medium speed, scraping the bowl often, until the mixture resembles coarse crumbs. Press the mixture evenly on the bottom of 3 greased and floured 9-inch round cake pans. Combine the cake mix, pumpkin, remaining butter, eggs and water in the same bowl. Beat at a medium speed, scraping the bowl often, until well mixed. Spread 1¾ cups of the batter over the crumbs in each pan. Bake for 20 to 25 minutes or until a toothpick inserted in the center comes out clean. Cool for 5 minutes and remove from the pans. Cool completely.

Combine the powdered sugar, ⅔ cup butter, cream cheese and vanilla extract in a small bowl. Beat at a medium speed, scraping the bowl often, until light and fluffy. Place one cake layer nut-side down on a serving plate. Spread with ½ cup of the filling mixture. Continue layering, using ½ cup of the filling mixture between the layers. Frost only the sides of the cake with the remaining filling. Spread the caramel ice cream topping over the top of the cake, drizzling some over the sides. Arrange the pecan halves in a ring on top of the cake. Refrigerate.

I first tasted this recipe at the home of Emilee Ward, a true hostess. I fell in love with this recipe. Emilee was kind enough to share it with me. Since then I have served it numerous times. There are never any leftovers! We used this recipe at a youth/adult bake-off at our church. It won the "Golden Whisk" award hands down.

Kim Mitchell

WOW: The house...should become the church of childhood, the table and hearth a holy rite.

Rev. Horace Bushnel, 1847.

Pineapple Refrigerator Cake

2 cups cake flour
1¼ cups sugar
3½ teaspoons baking powder
1 teaspoon salt
1 teaspoon grated lemon rind
½ cup shortening
1 cup less 2 tablespoons pineapple juice
1 teaspoon vanilla extract
3 egg whites

Sift the dry ingredients into a mixing bowl. Add the lemon rind.
Drop in the shortening. Add the pineapple juice and vanilla
extract. Beat for 2 minutes using an electric mixer. Add the egg
whites and mix well. Pour into two 8x8-inch pans. Bake at 350
degrees for 25 to 30 minutes. Let cool. Invert onto plates and
chill. Split the layers in half making 4 layers.

Pineapple Filling

¾ cup sugar
2½ tablespoons cornstarch
⅛ teaspoon salt
¼ cup lemon juice
Grated rind of one lemon
3 egg yolks, slightly beaten
2 tablespoons butter or margarine
16-ounce tub whipped topping

Combine all of the ingredients except for the whipped topping
in the top of a double boiler and stir until smooth. Cook over a
medium heat until thickened. Spread between the layers. Top
each layer with the whipped topping. Smooth the whipped
topping on the top and outside of the cake.

Kathryn Mitchell

Pineapple Upside-Down Cake

20-ounce can pineapple slices, drained, reserving juice
9 maraschino cherries
1 stick butter
½ cup light brown sugar
18½-ounce box yellow cake mix

Arrange the pineapple slices in the bottom of an electric skillet. Place one cherry in the middle of each pineapple slice. Heat the skillet and add the butter. Sprinkle the melted butter with the brown sugar. Prepare the cake mix according to the package directions substituting the pineapple juice for the water. Add enough water to the juice to make the correct amount of liquid. Spread the cake mix over the pineapples. Set the temperature to 350 degrees and cover. Check using a toothpick for doneness. Unplug the skillet. Score the sides of the cake using a knife. Invert onto a large plate or board.

When I was a small girl my mother, Jerl Dean Miller Adkins, baked her Pineapple Upside-Down cakes in an electric skillet to take to family gatherings and church homecomings. Years later this cooking technique came in quite useful.

After I married my husband, Pat, we had a doublewide trailer to burn down. We borrowed a friend's small trailer. It had a stove but the oven did not work. As time passed I had a craving for something sweet to eat such as a cake for our family. Without an oven the choices were limited. Then my memory kicked in and a cake popped out of my electric skillet, probably too many. Pat refuses to eat Pineapple Upside-Down Cake anymore!

Debra Hobbs Richards

Sour Cream Chocolate Cake
Cake

3 squares unsweetened chocolate
½ cup water
2 cups cake flour, sifted
1½ teaspoon baking powder
1 teaspoon baking soda
⅔ cup butter
1 cup sugar
⅔ cup light brown sugar
3 eggs
2 teaspoons vanilla extract
1 cup sour cream

Preheat the oven to 350 degrees. Combine the chocolate and water in a saucepan. Cook over a low heat, stirring until the chocolate melts. Place the pan in a bowl of cold water for about 2 minutes. Sift the flour, baking powder and baking soda in a bowl. Cream the butter and sugars in a separate bowl until light and fluffy. Add the eggs, one at a time, mixing well. Add the vanilla extract and sour cream and mix well. Add the chocolate mixture and flour mixture alternating between the two. Pour into floured and greased 9-inch cake pans. Bake for 30 to 35 minutes.

Frosting

3 squares unsweetened chocolate
2 tablespoons butter
¾ cup sour cream
¼ teaspoon salt
1 teaspoon vanilla extract
1-pound box powdered sugar

Combine the chocolate and butter in a saucepan and melt over a low heat. Let cool. Cream the sour cream, salt, vanilla and powdered sugar in a bowl. Add the chocolate mixture and mix well. Frost between the layers and the top of the cake.

This recipe has always been a favorite of mine. It is one of my first experiences in the kitchen with my mother, Sue Greene, who died in 1991. I remember so many of the special details she taught me about making cakes.

Donna Greene Hardesty

Spradling Cake

CAKE

⅔ cup butter
1½ cups sugar
2¾ cups all-purpose flour
2½ teaspoons baking powder
1 teaspoon salt
¼ cup cherry juice
¾ cup milk
½ cup chopped black walnuts
16 maraschino cherries, chopped
5 egg whites, stiffly beaten
1 teaspoon vanilla extract

Preheat the oven to 350 degrees. Cream the butter and sugar in a bowl. Sift the flour, baking powder and salt in a separate bowl. Add the dry ingredients to the butter mixture alternately with the cherry juice and milk. Stir in the nuts and cherries. Fold in the egg whites and vanilla extract. Pour the batter into two prepared 8 or 9-inch cake pans. Bake for 30 to 35 minutes.

Spradling Cake Icing

1 cup sugar
½ cup water
2 egg whites
¼ teaspoon cream of tartar
1 teaspoon vanilla extract

Combine the sugar and water in a saucepan. Boil until it makes an 8-inch thread in cold water. Beat the egg whites and cream of tartar in a bowl until stiff. Add the sugar syrup, gradually. Stir in the vanilla extract. Frost the cake.

I first ate this cake 50 plus years ago. My dad was friends with Clint Spradling and we would visit them occasionally. His wife, Nell, made this cake and we all loved it, but we didn't get the recipe until about 30 years later.

Elaine Mayes

Three-Day Coconut Cake

18½-ounce box yellow butter cake mix
6 or 7-ounce can flaked coconut
8 ounces sour cream
1½cups sugar
8-ounce tub whipped topping

Prepare the cake mix according to the package directions. Bake in two well-greased and floured 9-inch round cake pans. Combine the remaining ingredients and set aside. Remove the cake from the oven when done and let cool. Cut each layer in half length wise to make 4 layers.   Spread the topping between each layer, on the top and sides. Place the cake in the refrigerator in an airtight container for 3 days before serving.

Martha Ralph

Young Love...

Always remember today Aug. 17, 1933 (Thurs.) my boyfriend (Clarence Miller) and I went to the association at Zion. I've come back from the association by Clarence's home, and he gave me these leaves of an orange tree that they have in their yard (the first orange tree that I've ever seen). I'm keeping these leaves to remember this day by.

Velma

Traveling Sausage Cake

Cake

1 teaspoon baking soda
1 cup hot coffee
1 pound unseasoned sausage
1½ cups sugar
1 cup raisins
1 cup nuts
1 teaspoon cinnamon
1 teaspoon crushed cloves
1 teaspoon nutmeg
2½ cups all-purpose flour
1 teaspoon salt
1 teaspoon baking powder

My dad brought me this recipe. This cake traveled from Trimble County, KY up to north of Indianapolis and back down to Ohio County, KY.

Donna Ralph

Dissolve the baking soda in the coffee. Combine all of the ingredients in a bowl and mix well. Pour the batter into two greased and floured 9-inch cake pans. Bake at 325 to 350 degrees for 30 minutes. Cool.

Caramel Icing

¾ cup butter, melted
1½ cups brown sugar
6 tablespoons milk
1 pound powdered sugar

Combine the butter and brown sugar in a saucepan and boil for 1 minute, stirring constantly. Cool slightly. Add the milk and powdered sugar. Beat until smooth. Ice the cake. This icing does not harden and crack.

Vanilla Butter Nut Bundt Cake

Cake

2 cups self-rising flour
2 cups sugar
4 eggs
1 cup milk
1 cup cooking oil
2 teaspoons vanilla butternut flavoring

Combine all of the ingredients in a bowl and mix well. Pour the batter in a greased and floured bundt pan. Bake at 350 degrees for approximately 50 minutes.

Icing

½ stick butter
4 ounces cream cheese, room temperature
4 ounces powdered sugar
1 teaspoon vanilla butter nut flavoring

Melt the butter in a saucepan. Remove from the heat. Add the cream cheese and mix well. Combine the butter mixture, powdered sugar and vanilla butternut flavoring, mixing until smooth. Drizzle over the cooled cake.

This cake gets better the longer it sits...The recipe was given to me by one of my customers, Rachael Jackson, at my hair styling boutique in The Roosevelt House in Owensboro. She is a 6-year cancer survivor and a good Christian lady. She got the recipe from the late Lola May Neel, who was a resident of The Roosevelt House for 25 years.

Kitty Gray

In Loving Memory of
Esther Elizabeth Moseley
April 21, 1899 – August 31, 1980

This picture is the only one ever taken of my grandmother as a child. Esther Moseley was born before the turn of the 20th century, a fact that I found interesting as a small girl. Mamaw was a woman who had quiet, reserved mannerisms, a trait that her father, George Wilkerson, also possessed.

She witnessed the freezing over of the Ohio River in 1917 and skated across it with my grandfather. As a young woman, she drove a Model T and worked at Henrad in Owensboro. After she and Papaw married, she became a farmer's wife and the mother of seven sons, five of which were sent off to war. They say each time she bid a son farewell, she cried. Mamaw was a strong woman, though, and provided for her family well. Most all of the family's food was raised on the farm. I used to peek from behind the kitchen curtain to watch her wring a poor old chicken's neck. She hung them by their feet on a tree limb in the apple orchard.

She attended services at St. Mary of the Woods Catholic Church in Whitesville, for as long as she was able. I will always remember Mamaw as being old because by the time I came along her hair was gray and her arthritic fingers were quite gnarled. It was difficult for her to hold a knife in her hand to peel potatoes, but she never failed to cook a hot meal for the family. My favorite food was fried hamburger patties with homemade catsup. She didn't flatten her patties out like Mom does, she rounded them on top.

When she was placed in the rest home, my uncles visited her daily to make sure she was fed properly. Once when I visited, was sitting up in the bed calling the boys to dinner. She would fumble with the covers for awhile then peel potatoes for awhile, imaginary potatoes of course. Although her expression was motionless, I detected a twinkle in her eye as she called out the names of each of her sons.

Judith Ralph

Virginia and Artie's Molasses Layer Cake

Cake

1 cup molasses
2 tablespoons shortening, melted
1 teaspoon crushed cloves
1 teaspoon cinnamon
2½ cups all-purpose flour, sifted with a pinch of salt
1 teaspoon baking soda
1 cup boiling water

Combine the molasses, shortening, cloves and cinnamon in a bowl. Stir in the flour until stiff. Dissolve the soda in the water and add to the mixture. Pour the batter into two greased and floured 9-inch cake pans. Bake at 350 degrees for 25 minutes. Cool.

Raisin Filling

½ cup sugar
2 tablespoons flour or cornstarch
2 cups ground raisins
1 cup water
1 cup finely chopped almonds
1 cup finely chopped orange gumdrops

Combine the sugar and flour. Combine the sugar mixture and raisins in a saucepan. Add the water and stir to dissolve. Cook, stirring constantly, until thickened. Add the gumdrops and cook for 3 minutes. Add the almonds. Cool. Spread between the two cake layers.

BOILED ICING

1 tablespoon vanilla extract
4 cups sugar
4 cups milk
Lump of butter, about the size of a walnut

Combine all of the ingredients in a large saucepan. Cook to the soft-ball stage. Spread the icing on the top and the sides of the cake. Sprinkle the top with chopped butternuts.

I got this recipe when the family tore down the old Crowe home place. It belonged to Virginia and her mother, Artie.

Brenda Ambrose

PASS THE PUDDING PLEASE

When we kids were at home, my sister, Rosemary, did all the cookin'. You see, Mama worked. For Sunday dinner when all the family came to the house there were about 20 of us. We ate what we had around the house. My sister would make a great big pan of bread pudding. She tried cranberries in it, but I liked it best with raisins. When she passed that big pan of pudding we said, "You sure couldn't float down the creek with this, you'd sink first." It took a lot of food for our family.

Brenda Ambrose

PIES

Lois Elaine Lamar Brown and Hunter Brown
on their wedding day.

Anna's First Cookbook

My mother's first cookbook cost five dollars and was a wedding gift from her sister Myrtle Leach Craig. Inside the cover she made the following notes:

To: Shelia Joann Thurman

My first cookbook. Took with me to Hattiesburg, Mississippi in 1942. Hubert and I married Dec. 26, 1941. He was in the army in Hattiesburg, Miss. I went down there in 1942 to live. I went on the bus. I took my cookbook with me. I made out a grocery list while riding the bus. When I arrived, Hubert met me at the bus. We hired a taxi to take us to a Piggly Wiggly grocery store. We had two large brown bags of groceries for $5.00. I cooked lots of meals from this book.

The first meal I cooked in Hattiesburg was from this book. It was meatloaf, mashed potatoes and biscuits. The biscuits turned out "hard as rocks." I had unknowingly bought straight grade flour instead of self-rising. I decided I would make a pecan pie from the pecans I had gathered from across the road. My landlady told me to put a pan of water under the pie so it wouldn't burn. It was a kerosene oven. I took her at her word and set the pie directly in the pan of water and boiled the pie. Hubert told all his army buddies at Camp Shelby. From then on I was teased about boiling a pie.

Love,
Mama
(Anna Mary Leach)

Submitted by Shelia Thurman

App-ealing Apple Crumb Pie
Filling

4 large tart apples, peeled and sliced
9-inch pie crust, unbaked
½ cup sugar
1 teaspoon cinnamon

Topping

½ cup sugar
¾ cup self-rising flour
⅓ cup butter

Arrange the apple slices in the pie crust. Combine the sugar and cinnamon in a small bowl. Sprinkle over the apple slices. Sift the sugar and flour in a bowl. Cut in the butter until crumbly. Sprinkle over the apple slices. Bake at 400 degrees for 40 to 50 minutes.

Kellie Hall Ralph

Holidays with the Fuquas

One thing is for sure, when the Fuqua family gets together for the holidays we always have Mamaw Ruby's fruit salad and chocolate pie. We asked Mamaw to share her recipe, but she said she doesn't measure anything; she just throws it all together. When she is gone there will be no more.

Kellie Hall Ralph

Applesauce Pie

16-ounce can applesauce
½ cup sugar
½ stick butter or margarine
Cinnamon to taste
Two 9-inch unbaked pie crusts

Preheat the oven to 350 degrees. Combine all of the ingredients in a saucepan and heat over a medium heat until the butter is melted and the flavors blended. Pour into one of the unbaked pie crust. Top with the remaining pie crust, making slits in the top crust. Bake for 20 to 25 minutes until golden brown.

In a journal written by the late Lois Elaine Lamar Brown (my mother), she writes, "I don't remember what Mom fixed for dinner, but I wanted to fix something to show Hunter how good I could cook. They say 'The way to a man's heart is through his stomach.' I made a cream pie and just before I poured it in the pie crust, I reached in the closet to get the vanilla, didn't even look at it, and poured a big dash in the pie filling. I got one whiff and knew right away that I had grabbed the liniment bottle instead of the vanilla. I didn't serve that pie to him. I was sick over it. Another point lost!"

That story brings me to my favorite pie that my Mom used to make us. We were a family of nine, so we often ate simple foods, dishes that could be made quickly and would feed many. One of my most pleasant memories is when Mom would whip up her Applesauce Pie. I can remember each of us standing over her as she blended the ingredients together. I still remember the smell of that quaint kitchen with cinnamon and apples filling the air. Most often she would make at least two or three pies to feed the whole gang. We would anticipate those pies coming out of that oven. Mom would have to put them in the freezer to cool quickly because we just could not wait any longer. It was always nicely topped with a dollop of Cool Whip. How I long for one more piece of her authentic Applesauce Pie.

Apparently, she won over my Daddy's heart because he was more in love with her the day she went on to be with the Lord, sixty-one years later, than he was when she put the liniment in his pie.

Gaye Brown Swihart

Aunt Ruby's Chocolate Pie

1½ cups sugar
4 heaping tablespoons cocoa
½ cup all-purpose flour
1½ cups milk, scalded
3 tablespoons margarine
1 teaspoon vanilla extract
3 eggs yolks
9-inch deep-dish pie crust, baked

Combine the sugar, cocoa and flour in the top of a double boiler. Add the remaining ingredients, except the pie crust, and cook over a medium heat until thick. Pour the mixture into the pie crust.

Meringue

3 egg whites
½ teaspoon cream of tartar
¼ cup plus 2 tablespoons sugar

Beat the egg whites and cream of tartar on a high speed using an electric mixer for 1 minute. Add the sugar, 1 tablespoon at a time, beating until stiff peaks form and the sugar dissolves, about 2 to 4 minutes. Spread the meringue over the pie filling sealing to the edge of the pastry. Bake at 350 degrees for 10 to 12 minutes or until golden brown.

"I got this recipe from my Aunt Ruby. My mother died when I was 4 1/2 years old. We went to live with Granddaddy and my 3 'old maid' aunts. Aunt Ruby became my second mother until my daddy remarried 5 years later. When I would come back to visit my aunt, I would first go see my daddy then head straight to my Aunt Ruby's. The first thing I did was go to the refrigerator and I knew that there would be a chocolate pie waiting for me. I love this recipe because I loved my Aunt Ruby."

Jane Shaw

Blackberry Dumplings

1 quart fresh blackberries, rinsed
Water
Sugar

Dumplings

2 cups self-rising flour
3 tablespoons shortening
¾ cup milk

Place the blackberries in a saucepan. Add enough water for desired syrup and sugar to desired sweetness.   Cook the blackberries for about 30 minutes. Combine the flour, shortening and milk in a bowl. Spoon the mixture into the blackberries and cook until they are done. Serve by themselves or with a scoop of ice cream on top.

Melinda Schneider

Son

When I was about 3 years old, I spotted a ladder that Pap had left propped up against the front porch roof. Mam was in the kitchen washing clothes and I was outside. There was a limb hanging over the roof that was full of ripe peaches. I thought that I would climb up the ladder, walk across the roof, get the peaches and climb back down. And, that is what I did. Then, I carried them in the house to show Mam. She asked where did you get those peaches and I told her. Well, she said that if I went back up there I would get a switchin'...So, back around the house I went. Mam followed, but I didn't get the spanking that was promised. You see, I was SON!

James Lexter Leach

Heath Bar Pie

⅓ cup caramel ice cream topping
6-ounce graham cracker crust
1½ cups milk
3.4-ounce package vanilla instant pudding
8-ounce container whipped topping
6 Heath candy bars, broken

Spread the caramel topping onto the bottom of the graham cracker crust. Combine the milk and pudding in a bowl. Fold in the whipped topping. Stir in the candy bar pieces. Pour the mixture into the pie crust. Refrigerate any leftovers.

Kim Mitchell

When I think of the women who have made a difference in my life, the first one who comes to mind is my mom, Elza. She showed me as well as taught me how to love my family unconditionally. She sacrificed everything for us. She never had anything bad to say about anyone. This was confirmed at her funeral when many said, "Elza Motley never had a bad word to say of anyone."

Judy Back

Irish Potato Pie

Cook 2 medium potatoes, with jackets on, until tender. Peel and mash. Add ¼ stick butter. Beat 3 eggs with 1½ cups of sugar until well beaten. Add 1 teaspoon vanilla. Then add to mashed potatoes. Put in unbaked pie shell. Bake at 350 degrees for 35 minutes.

This recipe (in original form) was given to me at my wedding shower in 1962. Mrs. Otha Payne gave it to me. She was a member at Zion Church for many years.

Myrl Ralph

No Fuss Fixin's

When I was growing up I spent a lot of time at Granddad and Grandma Matthew's house. Grandma always had a spread of food laid out on the table. No matter when you stopped in, it looked like she had prepared for company. She had custard pies cooked every day, the old fashioned kind you put meringue icing on with yellow bubbles coming up through it. It would "tick" her off if "passer bys" did not stay to eat with the family...I have spent the night when she had as many as 39 family members for breakfast. She got up, fixed a big breakfast of bacon, eggs, ham, biscuits, gravy and whatever was available on the farm plus a bowls of cereal. Granddad would go to the Falls of Rough and come back with a bag full of groceries and a big tall box of Post Toasties. That was our special treat.

Grandma did all that cooking, made coffee, and had everything ready before she called anyone to the table. She could do it the easiest of anyone that I have ever seen. There was never any fuss or commotion. She just did it. My daughter-in-law, Lisa, is kind of like that. You would think she was doing nothing at all but the next thing you know, food is on the table.

Norman Matthews

Kitty's Blackberry Cobbler

1⅓ cups sugar
1 stick butter
1 cup self-rising flour
¾ cup milk
2 cups blackberries

Combine 1 cup of the sugar and butter. Add the flour and mix well. Add the milk and blend well. Combine the berries and the remaining sugar in a saucepan and heat until the sugar is dissolved. Pour the batter into a 1½-quart casserole dish. Pour the hot berries over the top. Bake at 350 degrees for 30 to 35 minutes or until golden brown.

My good friend, Kay Thornberry, and I were horse back riding one afternoon when we spotted a blackberry thicket. We rode our horses right up to the bushes and were able to pick the berries while mounted. We filled a couple of plastic shopping bags with the well-ripened blackberries and hung them on our saddle horns. All would have been well had we not decided to go riding around The Loop. To our surprise when we returned home our shopping bags were full of blackberry juice...I suggested to Kay, "Let's use the blackberries anyway." Guess what? We actually made a right nice cobbler that day!

Kitty Gray

WOW: Having a place to go is home. Having someone to love is family. Having both is a blessing.

Katherine Bailey

Lorene's
Chocolate Cream Pie

Filling

1½ cups sugar
½ cup cocoa
3 tablespoons cornstarch
3 cups milk
3 egg yolks, beaten
1 tablespoon butter
1½ teaspoons vanilla extract
9-inch pie crust, baked

Combine the sugar, cocoa and cornstarch in a saucepan. Bring to a boil and boil over a medium heat, stirring constantly until thick. Remove from the heat. Add the egg yolks and blend. Return to a boil and boil for 1 minute. Blend in the butter and vanilla extract. Pour into the pie crust.

Meringue

3 egg whites
6 teaspoons sugar

Beat the egg whites for 3 minutes. Add the sugar gradually and beat for 5 minutes until stiff peaks form. Spoon the meringue over the filling and seal the edges. Brown at 400 degrees for 6 to 8 minutes.

Where's the Chocolate?

One day my sisters, Velma Miller and Lorene Wright, and I decided to go blackberry picking on the Miller farm. We thought the pasture field would be the best place to pick berries. The cows had kept the weeds and grass down by grazing. They didn't bother the blackberry vines because they are very sticky briars. We picked a lot of berries and late in the day a big bull chased us! It was time to leave then and go home.

We were tired and hungry so went to Velma's house to cook supper. Velma and Lorene did the cooking. They knew how much I liked chocolate pie, my very favorite, so they made some for dessert.

Afterward they brought out a whole pie, wrapped in aluminum foil, just for me to take home. I was so excited to have a whole pie. I returned home and opened the pie, I was horrified! It was a dry "cow pile" from the pasture where we had picked berries. I was so disappointed! I called them up and told them so. Velma felt so bad about pulling the trick on me, that she made me a real chocolate pie every time we had family get-togethers. After Velma passed away in 1974, Lorene took up the tradition and made a chocolate pie for me each time we had get-togethers.

Through the years I have enjoyed countless delicious chocolate pies as a result of that one prank. So the joke was actually on them.

Anna Mary Leach

Mamaw Ruby's Oatmeal Pie

3 eggs, beaten
1 cup sugar
1 cup dark corn syrup
¾ cup old-fashioned oats
1 cup coconut
2½ teaspoons self-rising flour
¼ teaspoon vanilla extract
9-inch pie crust, unbaked

Preheat the oven to 450 degrees. Combine all of the ingredients in a bowl except for the pie crust. Pour the mixture into the pie crust and bake for about 5 minutes. Reduce the temperature to 350 degrees and bake until the pie is brown on the top.

Judith Ralph

Making Do

We used to eat everything but the legs off the table...sorghum molasses. This was no joke, Mama would cook breakfast every morning...90 biscuits, 2 dozen eggs and a big bowl of gravy. When we lived in the old house, she cooked on this old stove that used coal in it. It was metal and had big burners on it. Mama's had six burners. And the oven, I swear, Mama had to prop the door up with a stick to keep it from falling open. We didn't have chairs at the table so we all sat on lard cans. I was little bitty and could barely get up on that lard can, but I loved it. I thought it was cool.

Connie Ralph Boling

Mommy's Cool 'N Easy Pink Pie

⅔ cup boiling water
3-ounce package strawberry gelatin
½ cup cold water
Ice cubes
8-ounce tub whipped topping
6-ounce graham cracker crumb pie crust

Combine the boiling water and gelatin in a large bowl, stirring for at least 2 minutes until the gelatin is completely dissolved. Combine the cold water and enough ice to measure 1 cup. Add to the gelatin, stirring until the ice is melted. Add the whipped topping, stirring until smooth using a wire whisk. Refrigerate for 15 to 20 minutes or until the mixture is very thick and will mound. Spoon into the crust. Refrigerate for 4 hours or overnight.

When my son Andy and his family, Heather and Austin, were living in our house we spent a lot of time in the kitchen cooking. We fixed tacos and barbecued pork chops, mashed potatoes, milkshakes and more. Andy says that he never really gets full he just gets tired of chewing. Heather and Austin enjoy eating also, especially sweets and Austin never tired of eating Mommy's pink pie.

Judith Ralph

Pineapple Pie

1 stick butter, melted
1¾ cups sugar
2 tablespoons self-rising flour
3 eggs
8-ounce can crushed pineapple, undrained
9-inch pie crust, unbaked

Cream the sugar, butter and flour in a bowl. Add the eggs, one at a time, beating well after each. Add the pineapple. Pour the batter into the crust. Bake at 300 degrees for about 45 minutes to 1 hour or until brown on top. Serves 8.

Anna Sue Ralph Greer

Awful!!!

When I eloped at the age of 16, I didn't have much experience at cooking. My older sister, Emogene, had helped Mama with most of the cooking. After marriage, I went to my first Thanksgiving gathering at my sister-in-law, Jackie Hobbs' house. I baked a pumpkin pie for the meal. I took out a piece of the pie for my dessert and the first bite tasted awful. I had left out a very important ingredient, the sugar. My father-in-law, Buck Hobbs, had eaten a whole piece but had not said a word because he didn't want to hurt my feelings.

Jerl Dean Adkins

Please Pass the Peanut Butter Pie

¾ cup sugar
¼ cup plus 2 teaspoons cornstarch
⅛ teaspoon salt
3 egg yolks, beaten
3 cups milk
1½ tablespoons butter or margarine
1 cup creamy peanut butter
9-inch pie crust, baked

MERINGUE

3 egg whites
½ teaspoon cream of tartar
¼ cup plus 2 tablespoons sugar

Combine the sugar, cornstarch and salt in a heavy saucepan; stir well. Combine the egg yolks and milk and gradually stir into the sugar mixture. Cook over a medium heat, stirring constantly, until the mixture thickens and boils. Boil for 1 minute, stirring constantly. Remove from the heat. Add the butter and peanut butter and stir until thoroughly mixed. Pour into the pie crust and let cool.

Combine the egg whites and cream of tartar and beat at a high speed, using an electric mixer, for 1 minute. Add the sugar, 1 tablespoon at a time, beating 2 to 4 minutes or until stiff peaks form and the sugar dissolves. Spread the meringue to the edge of the pastry. Bake at 350 degrees for 10 to 12 minutes or until golden brown.

Judy Back

Simply Apple Dumplings

Two 8-ounce cans crescent rolls
2 cooking apples
2 sticks margarine
1½ cups sugar
1 teaspoon cinnamon
12-ounce can Mountain Dew

Separate the crescent rolls into 16 triangles. Peel and core the apples and cut into 8 slices each. Place 1 apple slice in each triangle of dough and roll up from large end to small. Place the rolls in a 9x13-inch pan. Melt the margarine. Add the sugar and cinnamon. Pour the mixture over the dumplings. Pour the Mountain Dew over the top. Bake at 350 degrees for 45 minutes or until brown. Serves 16.

The family loves this apple dumpling recipe for large gatherings. A little ice cream on top makes them extra good!

Ann Coppage

My wonderful grandmother, Edna Nugent, always said to keep my nose clean and I would always have a good reputation. This has always stuck with me. She was a wise Christian woman who loved the Lord with all her heart.

Sharon Vandgrift

Minnie Leach and
Rhoda Alice Wright,
Jerl Dean Miller,
Thelma Wright,
Emogene Miller

Thelma's Remembering....

My grandma Wright did not own a lot of property or have a lot of money, however, she overflowed with love and goodness! I loved her very much and felt her love in return. It was a major event for me to get to go to her house or her come to my house for a visit. It was such a joy to be near her. She was full of fun and would play games with me. She would sometimes play a card game called "I Doubt It." In the game the player had to call out numbers in consecutive order as they laid the card face down on the table. If someone challenged the card with, "I doubt it," then the card was revealed. If the card was what the person said it was the doubter had to take all the cards on the table. If the card was not what the person said it was, then they had to pick up all the cards. Grandma Wright couldn't stand to tell a little fib even if it was part of the game. She would get the giggles and say, "but I doubt it." Needless to say I won quite often.

Grandma knew how well I liked pork chops. So when she had pork chops for lunch or dinner, I did too! When she fried the chops she would wrap one or two in waxed paper then in two or three sheets of newspaper and stuff them in a brown paper bag. She would send them to me via Grand pap Wright. Grand pap's only means of transportation was walking. Even though we lived on opposite ends of town (about a mile apart) the chops would still be warm when he delivered them.

My grandmother Leach, whom I called Mom, lived in the country when I was small. I also loved her very much! I do not remember Mom playing games with me, but I loved to go visit her and have her visit us. She would let me play in her drawers and closets! That was always so fascinating to me getting to rummage through those drawers!

Mom often made me clothes when I was small. I remember one time she was making me a couple of new dresses; so naturally I occupied myself by playing in the machine drawers. I had been through all the drawers on that sewing machine several times when I picked up a pretty pink button and showed it to Mom. I said, "Mom this is what I have been looking for all this time!" Mom gave a little chuckle and said, "Well Honey, I sure am glad you found it!" Looking back, I am sure I was in her way and was getting on her nerves. But she had lots of patience and never let me know. That's one of the many reasons Mom Leach made an impression on my life.

Both of my grandmothers taught me to love God, study His word, go to church and pray Grandma Wright kept her Bible on the table next to her favorite rocking chair. She read her Bible daily actually many times a day. Mom Leach got on her knees beside her bed every night and she prayed partially aloud and partially in a whisper for at least thirty minutes and many times much longer. She always prayed for forgiveness, mercy, strength, praises, and blessings and for many many people by name that she knew and loved. Mom took me to church with her when Mother and Daddy did not go. Early in life my grandmothers helped me to recognize the power in knowledge of the Bible and God, as well as, the power of prayer and the feeling of security nestled in the love of God!

Thelma Wright Matthews

Sweets

OUR FAMILY (April 29, 2006)
(Front row) Julie Ralph Alford, Kellie Hall Ralph, Judith Ralph,
Austin Litsey and Heather Litsey. (Back row) Tyler McManaway, Jimmy Alford,
Nicholas McManaway, Robert Ralph, Dennis Ralph and Andy Ralph.

*You are the sweetest and most precious blessing in my life. No matter what the occasion, if one of
you is not present there is a void in my heart.*

LOVE MOM

Three Generations
Emogene Miller Moseley, Julie Ralph Alford, and
Judith Moseley Ralph, May 2006

If I could choose one special person to receive the "Granddaughter of the Year Award" it would be my daughter, Julie Ralph Alford. I am sure her grandparents would agree. Every week, Julie and her husband, Jimmy, take time out of their busy schedule to go to Papaw Ralph's house to fix supper and to play his favorite game of One-Eyed-Jack. This 86-year-old grandfather can hardly wait from one week to the next for their visit and relives each moment as if it were his last.

When Jimmy works the night shift, Julie packs her bags and spends the night with her Mamaw and Papaw Moseley in "her bedroom" just like she did when she was a child. Papaw Moseley watches by the window until she arrives and starts thinking up a bedtime snack for them. Julie never leaves home before eating supper with Jimmy. If she spends the night on Saturday night, she gets up early on Sunday morning and helps Mamaw Moseley prepare Sunday dinner. Julie is a caring and giving young lady and I am proud of both of them for supporting our family with so much love.

Mom
(Judith Ralph)

Auntie's Cream Candy

½ stick butter
5½ cups sugar
1 cup heavy whipping cream
½ cup cold water
Red and green food coloring
Peppermint or almond flavoring

Melt the butter in a saucepan. Add the sugar, milk and water. Bring to a boil, cooking over a low heat. Cook for 20 minutes. Test one drop of the mixture in a cup of cold water and if the drop can be picked up in your fingers and form a hard ball, the candy is ready. Divide the mixture in half and add one food coloring to each half. Add the flavoring to each half and mix well. Pour each portion on a marble slab and pull the candy until it becomes creamy. Slice and store in the refrigerator in an airtight container.

Take small amounts and make small open pea pods, putting tiny balls inside each pod to look like peas or form large flat buttons. This candy was given as Christmas gifts.

This recipe was given to Mama during World War II by her neighbor Ms. Auntie Surber. The method of preparing this candy was a very happy childhood memory because I got to help.

Dee Dee Ransdall

Chocolate Covered Marshmallows

24-ounce package chocolate almond bark
10-ounce package large marshmallows
Toothpick

Melt the chocolate almond bark in the microwave in a microwave safe bowl. Dip each marshmallow in the melted chocolate using a toothpick. Shake off any excess chocolate and place the marshmallows on a cookie sheet covered with waxed paper. Refrigerate until chocolate hardens. Mom doesn't put hers in the fridge, that's why mine are crispier. Serve in your favorite dish or tin.

I make these for my husband, Jimmy, for the holidays.

Julie Ralph Alford

"Mouse" in the Kitchen

When we were little, my brothers and I used to torment our mom (we wouldn't have done that if we didn't love you so much). One particular day we decided to pretend that we had caught a mouse in a big plastic container. Mom was washing dishes when we decided to let the "mouse" out, which was actually a stuffed baby kangaroo. We threw the "mouse" at Mom, she screamed and jumped up on the countertop almost in the dishwater. It was hilarious. There was never a dull moment in the Ralph's house.

Julie Ralph Alford

Darlene's No Chunks Strawberry Ice Cream

1 quart strawberries
Three 14-ounce cans sweetened condensed milk
Two 12-ounce cans strawberry nectar
12-ounce bottle strawberry soda
Three 12-ounce cans evaporated milk
¾ cup sugar

Place the strawberries in a blender to prevent chunks. Combine all of the ingredients in a large bowl and mix until smooth. Pour the mixture into an ice cream freezer cylinder. Add regular milk to the fill line. Freeze according to the directions with the ice cream maker.

Darlene Staples

Sunday Morning

When I was a kid Mama used to make us boys go to church on Sundays. She would load us up in a road wagon and set chairs up in the back. After church we would visit family, make ice cream and things like that.

Charles Moseley

Fruit Cookies

1 cup raisins
3½ cups all-purpose flour
1 teaspoon baking soda
1 teaspoon salt
1 cup shortening
2 cups brown sugar
2 eggs
½ cup sour milk
2 cups mixed fruit
½ cup cherries
1½ cups pecans

Preheat the oven to 400 degrees. Boil the raisins, drain and allow to cool. Sift the flour, baking soda and salt in a large mixing bowl and set aside. Combine the shortening, brown sugar, eggs and sour milk in a separate bowl and beat until creamy. Add the flour mixture and stir thoroughly. Add the mixed fruit, cherries, pecans and drained raisins. Drop by teaspoonfuls onto a greased cookie sheet. Bake for 10 minutes.

As far back as I can remember Mom would make this recipe every November. She would bake them and store them in Christmas tins. She would place a napkin on top of the cookies and an apple slice on top of the napkin. She had to make several tins to guarantee cookies at Christmastime. In 1990 Mom made her usual fruit cookies and stored them away. One year later, in November, Mom passed away. As we were going through her things, specifically her hutch, we found a leftover tin of those cookies hidden in the back. When we opened them they looked as fresh as the day Mom made them. They hadn't molded or decayed in any way. After opening them we cried, realizing this ended her tradition but.... I carry it on with my family."

Sheila Isaac
In memory of her mother Jean Motley

Mama Doolin's Sugar Cookies

2½ cups sugar
1 cup butter or lard
2 eggs
5 cups all-purpose flour
2 teaspoons baking powder
½ teaspoon nutmeg
¾ cup sweet milk
2 teaspoons vanilla extract

Cream the sugar and butter in a large bowl. Add the eggs and beat well. Sift the dry ingredients in a bowl. Add the dry ingredients alternately with the milk and vanilla extract and thoroughly combine. Roll out and cut with a floured biscuit cutter and place the cookies on a greased cookie sheet. Sprinkle each cookie with a small amount of sugar. Bake at 350 degrees for 8 to 10 minutes or until lightly brown. Do not over bake.

For a special treat Mama would make these best ever sugar cookies. She would stack them on a large platter and set them in the middle of the table. There was nothing better...they were so yummy! Mama was a good person and a wonderful cook. She made sure of two things at home, that you "had plenty to eat" and "plenty of cover." We will always cherish our memories. Hope you enjoy these cookies as much as we did then and still do!

Garnett Doolin Beatty

> *Mama was a good cook. That's all those older women did was cook...three hot meals a day, breakfast, dinner and supper.*
>
> *Billy Doolin*

Mammaw Lizzie's Teacakes

3 eggs, beaten
2 teaspoons vanilla extract
2 cups sugar
1 cup lard or shortening
½ teaspoon baking soda
1 cup milk
7 cups all-purpose flour
4 teaspoons baking powder

Combine the eggs, vanilla extract, sugar and lard in a large bowl and mix until smooth. Combine the baking soda and milk in a small bowl and add to the egg mixture. Sift the flour and baking powder in a separate bowl. Add the flour mixture slowly until the dough is the right texture for handling, not too sticky, not too dry and stiff. Roll the dough out on a lightly floured surface. Cut into rounds with a biscuit cutter or cookie cutters. Bake on an aluminum foil-lined pan at 350 degrees for 10 minutes.

Lizzie Mae Ralph Russell and her sister, Allie, often got up from an afternoon chat to make a dessert in Lizzie's spacious kitchen. By memory, they would pitch a little of this and a little of that into a bowl and within thirty minutes the wonderful aroma of something baking would float through the screen door, beckoning us to come in. Oh, for one of those wonderful teacakes to munch on again!!! They had the best flavor and were delicious served with a fresh glass of chilled milk. This recipe for teacakes is as near as I can get to having the original. Teacakes are of English origin and today we call them sugar cookies. The Ralph's are English and the original recipe was probably passed from generation to generation to use as a compliment to tea time.

Gail Lynn Russell Horn

Mammie's Toll House Cookies

2¼ cups all-purpose flour
1 teaspoon baking soda
1 teaspoon salt
2 sticks margarine, softened
¾ cup sugar
¾ cup brown sugar
1 teaspoon vanilla extract
2 large eggs
10-ounce package chocolate chips
1 cup chopped pecans

Preheat the oven to 350 degrees. Combine the flour, baking soda and salt in a small bowl. Beat the margarine, sugars and vanilla extract in a large mixing bowl until creamy. Add the eggs, one at a time, beating well after each. Beat in the flour mixture gradually. Stir in the chocolate chips and pecans. Drop by rounded table-spoonfuls onto ungreased baking sheets. Bake for 10 to 12 minutes. The cookies will be soft. Cool on the pan for 2 minutes. Makes approximately 4 dozen cookies.

My grandsons, Logan and Holten, and I started making these cookies before the oldest, Logan turned 2 years old. He is now 10 and they have both learned to read the recipe and measure the ingredients. The boys can now make the cookies by themselves even though I still bake them.

If the boys are out of school the first thing one of them will ask is "are we going to make cookies today?" I enjoy the time we spend together. I believe we are losing the art of doing simple things together as a family. I hope our cookie making tradition will always be a good memory for my grandsons.

Joan Cheek

Porter's Molasses Popcorn Balls

1 cup sugar
1 cup molasses
½ to ¼ cup vinegar
1 teaspoon baking soda

Combine all of the ingredients except the baking soda in a saucepan. Cook to a soft-ball stage. Stir in the baking soda. The mixture will foam. Pour over popcorn, stir and shape into balls. Place on waxed paper to cool.

Heather Litsey

Hickory Nut Cookies

½ cup sugar
1 cup butter
1 teaspoon vanilla extract
1 egg, slightly beaten
1 cup chopped hickory nuts or walnuts
2 cups self-rising flour

Preheat the oven to 350 degrees. Blend the sugar and butter in a bowl. Add the vanilla extract, egg and nuts and mix thoroughly. Stir in the flour. Spoon onto a lightly greased cookie sheet. Bake for 10 minutes.

Shirl and Sonja Back

Snowflakes

12-ounce package semisweet white chocolate morsels
½ cup butter
8 cups Crispix cereal
2 cups powdered sugar

Melt the chocolate morsels and butter in a large saucepan over a low heat. Remove from the heat. Pour the cereal into a large bowl. Pour the chocolate mixture over the cereal, tossing to coat. Pour the powdered sugar into a gallon-size plastic storage bag. Add the coated cereal to the bag, close and gently shake until the cereal looks snow white. Makes 9 cups.

Every Christmas Mama (Shelia Thurman) makes snowflake treats just for me. I eat the whole bowl!

Brandon Thurman

Brenda's Birthday 1962:
(Back Row) Anna Leach Oliver with daughters, Brenda, Janice
and (Front Row) Shelia

The Best Christmas Cookie

1½ cups powdered sugar
1 egg
1 cup margarine
1½ teaspoons vanilla extract
2½ cups all-purpose flour
1 teaspoon cream of tartar
1 teaspoon baking soda

Cream the powdered sugar, egg, margarine and vanilla extract in a large bowl. Add the flour, cream of tartar and baking soda and mix well. Chill for 2 hours. Roll out and cut in Christmas shapes. Bake at 375 degrees for 7 to 8 minutes. Decorate with your choice of icings, sprinkles, etc.

This recipe came from Phyllis Blanton. She babysat for me, when Michael and Kim were small, along with her children. We have made these cookies since then and it has become a tradition in the family. A week or so before Christmas I would get all of the ingredients together and let the kids know we were going to have a Christmas cookie baking party. They would watch while I mixed up the cookies. While they were chilling we would get the icing ready. Of course, we had to have every color imaginable that could be made from combining our basic colors. We would have sprinkles, chocolate jimmies, silver candy decorations and anything else edible we could find in the kitchen. As the cookies cooled we would mix everything up and get our stations ready. Then the fun would begin. There was always a contest for the prettiest cookie (the winner got to eat it) and for the ugliest one (daddy had to eat that one). There have never been more beautiful angels, stars, reindeer, Christmas trees and Santa's. I made the cookies with my children Michael, Kim and Karen until Kim got married and had a child of her own, Micki Shae. She took over the tradition and it has continued. She brings her dad a box of cookies every Christmas morning and he really looks forward to it.

Keni Spradling

Wendy's Frosty Ice Cream

½ gallon chocolate milk
8-ounce tub whipped topping, thawed
14-ounce can sweetened condensed milk

Combine all of the ingredients in a large bowl. Pour into an ice cream freezer cylinder. Freeze according to the freezer directions.

Anetta Mollohan

Letting Go

Thelma Marie and Norman were married 6 years before my only grandchild, Lawrence, was born. They lived in Louisville, KY and Paul and I couldn't wait to get up there to see our baby. We would head to Louisville every Saturday afternoon as soon as I got off from work. Paul would have the car packed and ready to go...Once when we got there, they had been invited to Norman's sister's house for supper. They didn't go because we showed up. After I found out, I told Paul we were going to have to stop going so often and let those kids live their life. It is so hard for a mother to let go.

Lorene Leach Wright

SISTERS

Years ago my parents divorced and my dad and I moved in with my grandparents. All I had was what was on my back. My dad felt bad for me so he bought me a TV, a pony and numerous other things to compensate for my loss.

As time went on, he met a wonderful woman who had a daughter that was two years older than me and much bigger. Eventually Dad and Geraldine fell in love and got married. We continued to live with my grandparents until Dad built another house on the farm.

It didn't take me long to figure out that there was one small word that I did not like and it was SHARE. The one thing that I really did not want to SHARE was Billy, my pony. However, my grandmother told me one day that I had to take my new sister for a ride. She did not know how to ride nor guide, so I had to lead her around.

We had gone out the lane towards the barn and were on our way back when we got to the garden. I decided to tie the bridle to a fence post that had a hornet's nest in it. Needless to say Billy got to moving around and got the hornets all stirred up and out they came. Billy got to bucking and, you guessed it, there went my sister flying to the ground. Of course she went screaming to the house and told on me and when my dad got home and found out what I had done, I didn't sit down for awhile.

Even though I did mischievous things to my sister back then, today she does wonderful things for me. So, we really did grow to love each other even though we weren't blood kin.

Carol Estes

Canning

Joyce Brothers Robinson

Joyce loved her gardening; she especially loved to grow beautiful flowers. She grew the prettiest Dinner Plate Dahlias you ever saw.

Kathryn Mitchell, mother

Corn Relish

3 dozen large ears corn, cut from cob
4½ cups vinegar
16 onions, chopped
1 large head cabbage, shredded
4½ cups sugar
6 teaspoons salt
6 red peppers, chopped
6 green peppers, chopped
1 quart mustard

Combine all of the ingredients in a large stock pot and cook until thick. Ladle into jars and seal.

The late Gladys Ralph's recipe
Submitted by Anna Sue Ralph Greer

THE BIG SECRET

During the winter months women used to gather at one another's house and sometimes us kids would be sent outside to play. I just knew they were talking about having babies and things like that. But kids today know more than their parents do!

Lorene Leach Wright

End of Garden Soup Mixture

8 medium potatoes, diced
16 carrots, diced
8 cups quartered tomatoes, peeled
4 cups cut green beans
4 cups fresh corn
4 cups chopped cabbage
8 quarts water
Salt

Place all of the vegetables and water in a large soup kettle and simmer for 2 to 3 minutes. Put 1 teaspoon salt in the bottom of each hot, sterilized jar. Pack with mixture and seal.

Brenda Ambrose

SEEDS OF LIFE

When I look back at the women who have influenced me and my decisions I find myself comparing them to sowing seeds. Mom, who actually started the whole gardening process by giving birth to me, is my gardener. My grandma Motley, who I spent many nights with, sowed the seeds of kindness. Mama never said anything unkind about anyone. I can't say I've inherited that meekness; I am reminded of her example each time I fail in that area. Mama Back sowed the seeds of hard work. She didn't believe in idleness. Mrs. Reed, a home economics teacher, who truly believed in me added fertilize for confidence. My lady friends have sewn the seeds of wisdom. The lessons I've learned by observing them will be life long. I owe a great debt to all those who have help me to grow as a woman, wife and mother.

Kim Mitchell

Ida B's
Green Tomato Ketchup

1 large head cabbage
½ peck green tomatoes, about 4 quarts
12 green hot peppers
12 green sweet peppers
3 pints vinegar
2 pounds sugar
½ cup salt
2 tablespoons turmeric
2 tablespoons mustard seed
1 tablespoon cinnamon
1 tablespoon allspice
1 tablespoon celery seed

Chop the cabbage, tomatoes and peppers in a food processor very coarsely. Place all of the ingredients in a large pot and cook for 30 minutes. Seal in hot jars. Store in a dark place until ready to open.

I have lots of good memories of eating at my house when all twelve of us kids were still home. It was such a warm feeling to smell the good food coming from the kitchen. The kitchen was a special place. We all liked to watch mama cook and to talk with her and laugh with each other. Mama would have a big kettle of brown pinto beans with some jowl bacon cooking and a large pot of mashed potatoes ready to eat along with a big iron skillet of corn bread. She would bring out a jar of her homemade "Green Tomato Ketchup." It was delicious to mix it in your beans or just put it to the side.

Garnett Beatty

Mama's Sweet Cucumber Pickles

1 quart cucumbers
Pickle seasoning
2 cups vinegar
1 cup sugar

Wash and slice or quarter the cucumbers. Soak the cucumbers in salt water overnight. Combine the pickle seasoning, vinegar and sugar in a saucepan. Bring to a boil and drop the cucumbers in. Return to a boil. Place the cucumbers in a quart jar. Fill with liquid and seal.

During the 1970's, I moved to a farm at Tick Ridge in Ohio County, KY. I planted a large garden with a lot of cucumbers. When it came time to pick them, I wondered how I would ever get all those cucumbers made into pickles. All of the recipes in the canning books took so many days to process. I was desperate as I had other fresh vegetables to take care of. Like all daughters in need, I called my mother, Minnie Leach. She had the very recipe I needed. It was the one she used when she was raising us five children. I have never seen this recipe in a book, but I remember how much I enjoyed Mama's sweet pickles.

Anna Mary Leach

Good Name

Mama was a good sweet mother. She always wanted us to do the right thing and when we were young she set a good example. Mama told us if you're poor and don't have anything worldly and you lose your good name, you have lost everything.

Lorene Leach Wright

Mammy's Green Tomato Relish

½ bushel green tomatoes
2 large heads cabbage
20 onions
24 peppers
1 gallon vinegar
5 pounds sugar
Salt to taste
3 tablespoons pickling spice, tied in a cloth

Chop the tomatoes in a food processor and drain. Chop the cabbage, onions and peppers in the food processor. Combine all of the ingredients in a large pot. Bring to a good boil and cook until the vegetables change color. Spoon into quart jars and seal. Makes 15 quarts.

I stayed a lot with my grandmother, Lilly Petty Thurman, when I was a kid. We called her Mammy. She was a good, kind and loving grandmother. She used to make the best green tomato relish. It made pinto beans and corn bread really taste good. We also used this for relish on hot dogs and even mixed it with mayonnaise and a little sugar to make tartar sauce for fried fish.

Roger Thurman

WOW: Pretty is as pretty does.

The late Minnie Bell Basham Leach

Squash Pickles

6 cups sugar
4 tablespoons celery seeds
2 tablespoons salt
4 tablespoons mustard seeds
4 cups vinegar
4 large bell peppers, chopped
4 cups chopped onion
16 cups thinly sliced yellow squash
8 ounces chopped pimentos, optional

Combine the sugar, spices and vinegar in a saucepan and bring to a boil. Add the remaining ingredients and stir. Bring back to a rolling boil and cook for approximately 5 minutes. Lower the heat and dip the mixture into hot jars and seal. Place in a hot water bath and process for 10 minutes. Good with dried beans and corn bread. Makes 5 quarts and 1 pint or 11 pints.

Pamela Ralph Howard

Corn Bread without Milk

My husband taught me how to cook corn bread without milk. One night I was going to cook corn bread and didn't have any milk. I was going to send someone out to buy a gallon of milk when Phil said, "Sandy you don't have to have milk to make cornbread. Just substitute an equal amount of cream-style corn for the milk." I did and it was good. But, you have to remember to use cr eam-style, not whole kernel corn.

Sandy Harrington

Velma's Lime Pickles

7 pounds cucumbers
2 cups lime
2 gallons cold water
9 cups sugar
1 teaspoon celery seed
1 teaspoon whole cloves
2 quarts white cider vinegar
2½ tablespoons salt
1 teaspoon pickling spice

Wash and thickly slice the cucumbers. Combine the lime and water and soak the cucumber slices for 24 hours, stirring often. Rinse using clear water. Soak the cucumbers in plain water for 3 hours and drain. Combine the remaining ingredients and soak the cucumber slices overnight. Heat the mixture slowly. Bring to a boil, reduce the heat and simmer for 25 minutes. Dip the pickles into warm jars and seal while hot. Makes 20 pints.

This is the lime pickle recipe that Mamaw Miller used. She passed away at age 57 in 1974. We canned 40 pints of lime pickles that year.

Judith Ralph

Anna Mary Leach, Myrtle Leach Craig, Velma Leach Miller
holding Emogene, Lorene Leach Wright holding Thelma

FAMILY VALUES...

I am thankful for the women that have had influenced me in a positive way con-
cerning family and moral values. I looked forward to holidays and special occasions
with so much excitement when I was a child. We had get-togethers with delicious
potluck meals prepared by the many great cooks in our family circle.

We had Christmas dinner at my Grandmother Leach's home. She cared very deeply
about her family and always set a good example. She never said a bad thing about
anyone and never complained about anything. Even though she had her share of
hard times and heartaches, she never lost her faith. She read her Bible every day.
I remember her sitting in the front porch swing during the summer with a Bible in
her lap. In the wintertime she would be rocking beside the Warm Morning heater
reading the Bible with the family prayer list in hand.

My Grandmother Flora Miller also cared very much about her family. She was a
widow when her son, my dad, married my mother. My sister, brother and I were

her only grandchildren. She never drove a car but lived within walking distance of
Fordsville, KY and of our house. My mother raised a big garden and Grandmother
Miller would walk down to help in the canning. She and Grandmother Leach, as well
as my mother quilted.   My mother pieced quilt tops from material scraps from the
clothing she had made for herself, my sister and me. Grandmother Leach and
Grandmother Miller quilted some of them for her. They quilted for income and made
quilts for themselves and family. My dad, Clarence Miller, said that Grandmother
Miller had made latch hook rugs to sell in her earlier years.

My mother, Velma Leach Miller, was very dedicated to her family. She was a very
good cook and always had cake, cookies or some other goodies on hand, just in case
someone stopped by. Everyone in our family loved to visit her house. I developed
my interest in cooking from watching and helping her. When I was old enough, I
began making cakes from the recipes on the back of the 5-pound flour sacks. I
would also get recipes from the Progressive Farmer Magazine. When I was a young
girl we had chickens for eggs and to eat, a milk cow for fresh milk and butter and
hogs for pork. We did not depend on the grocery store for all of our food supplies.
Mama was a loving and caring Grandmother to all of her grandchildren. Some of
my son and daughter's best childhood memories are of the times spent with her.

Mama has long since passed and we now have our Leach and Miller family get-
togethers on our farm in the old farmhouse where I was born that my husband and
I restored.

My daughter, Judith Ralph, co-author of this book is a loving mother and has always
put her family first. Her daughter, my granddaughter, has always been interested in
watching and helping me cook. She is now an excellent cook. She also has the love
of family and helps me prepare meals for the holidays, especially Thanksgiving. I
hope these family values and moral values will continue throughout the generations
to come.

Emogene Miller Moseley

MISCELLANEOUS

Ralph Family: (Back row) Andrew Ralph, Herman Ralph, Roy Ralph, Margaret Payne, Martine Ward, Lucille Farmer, William "Bease" (Front Row) J.W. Ralph, Jimmy Ralph, Allie Ralph and Eugene Ralph.

One thing I can say about my mother, Allie Ralph, is that she was a hard worker. She would get up at 2 and 3 o'clock in the morning, wash clothes on a wash board in a tub and have them hung out by daylight.

Roy Ralph

Through Grandma's Eyes

When I was pregnant with my first child, all indications looked as if a cesarean delivery was a definite possibility. I was scared to death and was hoping that I could avoid a surgical birth. Imagine my surprise when my grandmother was just thrilled that I was getting to have a cesarean delivery.

My maternal grandmother, Grace Ford, had nine children. My grandfather left her and the family when she was pregnant with her ninth child. I have often wondered how she managed to raise nine children by herself without any of the opportunities available to single mothers today. She was a working single mom long before it was a common practice. There were no child support payments or government programs to help her. She did it with hard work and faith in God. She worked daily in a factory and the older kids took care of the younger ones. My mother was the oldest, and my father was often a father figure to her younger siblings. I was only 3 1/2 years younger than my mother's youngest sister, so I just fell right in behind the others. I remember how hard she worked to take care of all of and raise them in the right way.

After having eight uneventful births, my grandmother's ninth child had to be delivered by cesarean. Back in the 50's, this meant a long extended stay in the hospital. My grandmother told me she hoped I would get a cesarean because it was the most rest she had ever gotten!

Pam Allard

Dry Rubs

Andrew's Dry Rub
O'Charley's Style

1 cup brown sugar
½ cup paprika
¼ cup kosher salt
¼ cup coarse-ground pepper
4 tablespoons Italian seasoning

Andrew's Memphis-Style Dry Rub

1 cup brown sugar
½ cup paprika
¼ cup kosher salt
¼ cup coarse-ground pepper
4 tablespoons Italian seasoning
1 teaspoon celery salt
1 teaspoon dry mustard
1 teaspoon onion powder
1 teaspoon garlic powder
1 teaspoon cayenne pepper

Andrew's Steak Dry Rub

2 tablespoons chili powder
2 tablespoons garlic powder
1 tablespoon cayenne pepper
½ teaspoon salt
½ teaspoon black pepper

Andrew's Brisket Dry Rub

2 tablespoons garlic powder
½ cup paprika
3 tablespoons sea salt
2½ tablespoons black pepper
3 tablespoons sugar
1 tablespoon chili powder

Andrew's Turkey Dry Rub

2 teaspoons chili powder
1 teaspoon ground cumin
1 teaspoon dried oregano
1 teaspoon garlic powder
2 teaspoons onion salt
¼ teaspoon ground allspice
¼ teaspoon cayenne pepper
2 tablespoons olive oil
2 tablespoons lime juice

Combine all of the ingredients for each dry rub recipe. Place in an airtight container until ready to use. Sprinkle the desired amount onto both sides of the meat and rub into the meat. Bake or grill.

Andrew Hollifield

Equivalencies

A pinch = ⅛ teaspoon or less
1 tablespoon = 3 teaspoons
4 tablespoons = ¼ cup
8 tablespoons = ½ cup
12 tablespoons = ¾ cup
1 cup of liquid = ½ pint
2 cups liquid = 1 pint
4 cups liquid = 1 quart
2 pints = 1 quart
4 quarts = 1 gallon
8 quarts = 1 peck, such as apples, pears, etc.
16 ounces = 1 pound

Some people like me that have not been cooking long need to know these things.

Heather Litsey

Runaway Vacuum Cleaner

Mamaw Miller always saved the vacuuming for when I came to visit. She had an old burgundy GE vacuum cleaner with a light on the front. The bag would blow up real big when she vacuumed and it would make a loud whining sound. I was scared to death of that vacuum cleaner and would run and jump behind the couch in the living room corner and hide. I thought I was safe back there.

Barry Moseley

Honey

45 rose petals
25 red clover blooms
25 white clover blooms
2 cups water
10 cups sugar
1 teaspoon alum

Wash and soak the petals in salt water and drain. Combine all of
the ingredients in a large pan. Bring to a boil and boil for 2
minutes. Strain into jars using a cheesecloth. Makes about
4 pints.

*I make this recipe even to this day. The local floral shop saves their discarded rose
petals for me. You must wait until the clover is in bloom before making honey.
This is the recipe Grandma Spradling and Aunt Nell used. Phyllis remembers going
with Mickey to stay with Grandma when they were young and she would have this
honey. They really looked forward to it. I have never seen another recipe for honey
and it is really good and easy to make.*

Keni Spradling

Minnie's White Wash

10 pounds salt
1 pound alum
1 bar soap
10 gallons water, divided
50 pounds slack lime

Dissolve the salt, alum and soap in a portion of water and heat. Soak the lime with the remaining water. Add the lime mixture to the soap mixture and stir. Let stand for 24 hours before using.

I was thumbing through my recipes when I found my mother's, Minnie Bell Basham, recipe for white wash. When I was growing up in the 1920's and 30's people white washed everything in their yards from tree trunks to fence posts to the outhouse. Papa Leach white washed the trees in our yard in the spring. This was the tradition until the 1960's. The idea was to make the yard look neat. We also swept the yard if the grass had worn off by children playing ball. My oldest sister, Myrtle, was so particular after sweeping the yard that she would not let my other two sisters, Velma and Lorene, bring their pretend "umbrellas," branches from a sassafras tree, into our yard. Myrtle was afraid that a leaf might fall from the "umbrella" and mess up the yard.

Anna Mary Leach

Leach Family: Minnie Bell Leach, Willie Leach, Myrtle Mayer, Lorene Wright, James Lexter Leach and Anna Leach

In Loving Memory of Minnie Bell Basham Leach
October 12, 1895 – August 31, 1985

My gentle little Grannie was very meek and very wise. Spending the night at Grannie's was always special. We would sit in the front porch swing and she would help me with my homework. Education was important to her. After we finished my homework she would play games with me. She always had the best vegetable soup waiting on the stove.

We would say our prayers before bedtime. She would have us get down on our knees beside her tall bed. This spoke of Grannie's strong faith and her humbleness to God. Mama said in about 1932 her older brother and sister, Lexter and Lorene were gravely ill with typhoid fever and the mumps. They almost died. Grannie and Papa started family prayers at night kneeling at the bedside during that time.

Years later when Grannie and I would get down on our knees together, I noticed how Grannie would struggle. She had the pain of arthritis in her legs but that did not stop her. She had a stroke at the age of 84 which left her partially paralyzed on the right side of her body. She would say "this is not of God," meaning her ill-ness. She was bedridden for the last 6 years of her life.

During that time her quite strength and unwavering faith taught me to persevere no matter what life hands you. God never leaves his children or forsakes them. I know that I will see Grannie again when we have our reunion in heaven. What a comfort!

Shelia Oliver Thurman

Index

Cakes

Canning

Main Dishes

Miscellaneous

Pies

Soups

Sweets